Editorial

At the time of writing, Brexit, departure of the United Kingdom from the European Union, dominates headlines on these islands and – if much less urgently – finds a place in political discussion and commentary elsewhere in Europe and even further afield. Increasingly, the Irish 'backstop' – the provision to keep the border between the North and the Republic open, whatever the outcome of the UK and EU's future relationship negotiations – is being presented as, if not the nub of the problem, then at least a major contributor to the ongoing difficulties being experienced on all sides. William Kingston argues quietly in these pages that Irish diplomacy and political strategy might actually have handled the matter differently and in a way that could have saved Theresa May's deal with the EU and spared us from the 'hard Brexit' approach now being pursued with vigour – some might say abandon – by her successor Boris Johnson, with possibly much more menacing implications for this island.

On the other hand, defenders of the necessity for insisting on the backstop and avoidance of a hard border, which its removal from any arrangement made in the immediate future would almost certainly ensure, include not only the Irish government and main opposition but all twenty-six remaining EU countries, who have been steadfast in their alignment with Ireland throughout the long and painful saga. They are convinced that peace in the North is far from secure, twenty years after the Good Friday Agreement of 1998. Fergus O'Ferrall, who recently served as Lay Leader of the Methodist Church in Ireland, in his contribution to the current issue of *Studies,* emphasises 'the continuing grave and unresolved situation on the island of Ireland'. Those familiar with life on the ground in the North, unlike the more strident Westminster Brexiteers judging glibly from afar, know only too well how fragile the peace remains. The recent shameful murder of the noble young journalist Lyra McKee in Derry was a shocking reminder of the dangers which still lurk beneath the surface of apparently restored normality. Warped thinking, malign motivations and deep distrust have not gone away.

There are many challenges from all the Churches here but surely few more pressing than the work of reconciliation and reconciliation in the first instance between those who profess a common belief in Jesus Christ. St Paul, in his second letter to the Corinthians, speaks of 'God, who reconciled us to himself through Christ and gave us the ministry of reconciliation'

(2 Cor 5:18). Exercise of this ministry is at the very heart of the Gospel in any circumstances and it is a continuing scandal that Christian communities remain what Bishop Richard Hanson long ago called 'captive Churches', in bondage to the past, faith and politics destructively enmeshed. In the continuing absence of functioning politics in the North itself and against the background of the unhelpful noises currently emanating from Westminster, the task of embarking with renewed commitment on this 'painful, risky, difficult journey' of reconciliation, to quote Dr O'Ferrall, is an arduous one but of the highest importance. His clarion call in the paper published here is most timely.

What the Brexit debate in the UK has consistently ignored is the role the EU (and its earlier incarnations) set out to play from the beginning in the work of reconciliation on a war-torn continent, a role it has played with signal success and which it continues to play today. At a time when the world is showing signs of growing division, such work is more urgent than ever. Much of the Brexiteers' campaign – waged in not a few instances by politicians who should and probably do know better – has focused on the defects of the EU, including what is often referred to as 'the democratic deficit'. The discussion in *Studies* of some of the demerits of what they call the 'hegemonistic' European Union by Ray and Maurice Kinsella and their call for greater autonomy for member-countries might appear, on superficial inspection, to buttress the case for Brexit and indeed from other forms of disaffiliation from the Union. This is not, in fact, the authors' intention but they are seriously concerned that 'the present crisis', as they put it, should be used as a means of halting the process whereby 'the locus of responsibility' has been progressively and damagingly shifted away from the *demos* in individual countries', so that it has become centralised, instead, 'within the control of the dominant countries'.

Gladys Ganiel, making a welcome response to the summer issue of *Studies* (CVIII, 430, 2019), contests what she sees as a too-bleak assessment of the impact of Pope Francis's visit to the World Meeting of Families in Ireland last August and produces valuable survey evidence in support of her own cautiously more upbeat judgement. The contention in the editorial and a number of the articles in that issue was that media focus had been too exclusively on the problem of clerical sexual abuse and they were critical of the ways in which this focus limited the visit's impact. For the present writer it remains a difficulty that such a filter has been in operation throughout the present pontificate in the Irish media, effectively editing out other and arguably larger contributions that Pope Francis has been making in a variety of areas, not least his large presence on the world stage as a relentless peacemaker and figure of reconciliation. For this, the Irish Church must itself take some of the blame – just how much effort have we made to communicate his message? What is certain, in any case, is that, in a world increasingly characterised by divisive political leadership and the erection of actual or metaphorical walls between fellow-human beings, too often in the form of the rich and powerful barricading themselves against the weakest and the poorest, such a voice as the pope's desperately needs to be heard by all of us.

Demonisation and exclusion of 'the other' is a heinously ugly feature of the kind of populist demagoguery which is the hallmark of a growing number of political leaders round the world, with a deeply regrettable headline being set in this regard in the United States. In his illuminating review here of former US Secretary of State Madeleine Albright's recent book on the global situation, revealingly entitled *Fascism – a Warning* (2018), retired Irish ambassador John Swift notes 'the broad similarities which link Trump with Mussolini and Hitler, especially his strident nationalism and his encouragement of popular anger, envy, resentment and fear'. Tellingly, in the context of the present discussion, Swift quotes her observation that 'it was fear that Fascism might return to the continent where it was born that spurred the drive for European integration'.

Hitler's ostracism and persecution of 'the other' in the 1930s and 1940s was deployed in a campaign of genocidal anti-semitism, which spread far beyond German borders at the time. Despite almost universally shared abhorrence of the Holocaust, anti-semitism persists in many places, always threatening to break out again and claim some kind of perverse legitimacy. Ireland has not always been immune from this disease. In the present issue of *Studies*, Shai Afsai contributes a fascinating discussion of the work of the relatively little-known Dublin poet and writer Gerry Mc Donnell. In 'A Persistent Interest in the Other: Gerry Mc Donnell's Writings on Irish Jews', he quotes some deeply moving, deeply troubling lines from his subject's poem 'The Missing', which merit quotation. The poem, as he writes, 'references Celtic mythology — suggesting a kinship between the Lost Tribes of Israel and the Irish — as part of a crushing critique of the way Irish bureaucracy prevented Jews from finding refuge outside Nazi-controlled Europe. Here it is French Jews who are missing, because they have been murdered:

The children of the tribe of Dan
of the Tuatha De Danann,
Esther in the middle
the twins David and Michael on either side
and Daniel in front of her
came to our door
and we closed it on them.
The birds stopped singing
and never sang again.

It's five to five on a Friday
close of business;
stamp the permit for God's sake!

The children of the tribe of Dan
of the Tuatha De Dannan
of Le Marais in Paris
went to school that morning
kissed by their mothers.
By lunch time
they were gone
in the thundering trucks.
Each child was chained to the other,
Esther in the middle
the twins David and Michael on either side
and Daniel in front of her.
When the silver chains were broken
they became withered people.
The birds stopped singing
and never sang again.

It's five to five on a Friday
close of business;
stamp the permit for the children's sake!'

John Swift ends his review in *Studies* of Madeleine Albright's book (which he combines with consideration of the Singaporean diplomat Kishore

Mahbubani's *Has the West Lost It? A Provocation*), with a powerful and sobering quotation from a survivor of the Warsaw Uprising. Stanislaw Aronson, now ninwty-three and living in Israel, wrote last September in *The Guardian* of – in Swift's words – 'his fears that extremism was rising again in Europe and elsewhere'. Pondering the lessons to be learnt from the terrible history he had experienced himself, he concludes: 'Finally, do not ever imagine that your world cannot collapse, as ours did. This may seem the most obvious lesson to be passed on, but only because it is the most important. One moment I was enjoying an idyllic adolescence in my home city of Lodz, and the next we were on the run. I would only return to my empty home five years later, no longer a carefree boy but a Holocaust survivor and Home Army veteran, living in fear of Stalin's secret police'. There are children in Syria and Yemen and too many other places who are replicating such experiences now, as I write these words.

Alexandra Slaby's thoughtful examination of 'The Christian Meditation Movement', originated by the Irish Benedictine monk, John Main, might seem a far cry from such solemn forebodings. But, as she points out from the very outset, prayer and faith, interiority and religious practice, are inextricably linked. She examines the teachings of the late Fr Main and his World Community for Christian Meditation to discern whether, with its promotion of the 'mantra' and other practices drawn from Eastern religions, such an approach to spirituality is in danger of diluting the authentic Christian tradition and lapsing into a form of Pelagianism. But, while warning that problems can exist for Christians 'meditating far from their spiritual base', she demonstrates that John Main's teaching and that of his disciple, fellow-Benedictine Laurence Freeman, is rooted in the hesychastic practice of the early desert monks. She quotes Main's *Word into Silence* (1988; 2006), where he reminds readers that 'in prayer we are not striving to make something happen. It has already happened. We are simply realising what already is'. Moreover, as we attend to the presence of Jesus Christ, who is 'Light and Life' within us, 'we pay attention to our own true nature, and by becoming fully conscious of the union of our nature with Christ, we become fully ourselves. By becoming fully ourselves we enter the fullness of life Jesus has brought us' This is authentic Christian prayer.

The point to be made here is that, without this dimension of interiority, Christianity is simply not itself, not faithful to the teaching and example of Jesus Christ and the work of reconciliation in his name has no true or solid foundation. For the great twentieth century German theologian Karl Rahner, religion is the dimension of depth in all human experience. Without reflective interiority and a prayer that aspires to what John Main describes, not the mere recitation of words, religion risks being mere ideology, or other things, but not the search for God which all true religion is about. The recently deceased Swiss actor Bruno Ganz, who played the part of Hitler in the celebrated 2004 film, *Downfall* (*Der Untergang*), once spoke of how he had looked forward to the role and 'getting inside Hitler', only to discover that 'there was no inside Hitler'. We may ponder with deep misgiving how much 'inside' there is in some of the politicians dominating the scene in our time.

Finally, among the main body of articles, Tim O'Sullivan reflects on an earlier issue of *Studies*, entitled 'The Nuns' Story: Writing the Record' (CVII, 427, 2018), which was designed to cast light on the positive contribution of religious sisters to the well-being of the world. Drawing on his own 2013 research, he highlights the work of religious, men and women, to healthcare in Ireland, which has been inadequately appreciated and about which, in his judgment, the voice of the religious themselves is in need of being heard. The public disparagement of nuns and the unjust misrepresentation of their motives in certain quarters in Ireland has been an aspect of how public discourse on Church-related issues has grown somewhat coarse in the most recent years in our country. Dr O'Sullivan's essay helps to correct the picture.

If there is a loosely unifying theme in this issue of *Studies*, which is disparate in its range of features, it is the theme of reconciliation. One of the most luminous figures of the twentieth century, now coming into greater prominence, is the young Dutch Jewess Etty Hillesum (1914–43). From what might be described as a standing start, in terms of her religious background, a non-practising, dysfunctional Jewish home, and growing up as the terrible shadow of Nazi barbarism fell over the Netherlands, by what might seem improbable paths she found her way, without the aid of conventional, institutional religion of any kind, into the most profound spirituality, which sustained her and helped her to sustain others around her in her turn as they confronted the inhuman horrors of Auschwitz, where she herself died, just twenty-nine years of age, in November 1943. Her story is lucidly told in Patrick Woodhouse's *Etty Hillesum: A Life Transformed* (2009). The diaries she had begun to keep, and which have only recently come to prominence, accurately reflect the extraordinary extent of her interior development. The last entry, written in September, contain these remarkable words: 'We must be willing to act as a balm for all wounds'. Those words should impose themselves on the hearts of all of us, above all of those who would be 'ministers of reconciliation' in this increasingly troubled world.

Excerpts from the work of Gerry Mc Donnell reproduced with kind permission of Lapwing Press.

Excerpts from *Words into Silence. A Manual for Christian Meditation* reproduced with kind permission of Canterbury Press.

Corrigendum: In *Studies* CVIII,430 (2019), on the Contents page, the review of Ivan Gibbons's *The British Labour Party and the Establishment of the Irish Free State, 1918-1924*, was incorrectly ascribed to David Walsh. The review was written by John Swift.

Cover image: Collage / Shutterstock

Irish Churches and Reconciliation: Breaking the Bondage of the Past

Fergus O'Ferrall

Bear in mind these dead:
I can find no plainer words ...
The careful words of my injunction
are unrhetorical, as neutral
and unaligned as any I know:
they propose no more than thoughtful response.[1]

John Hewitt

The current situation

The continuing grave and unresolved situation on the island of Ireland calls all who acknowledge Jesus Christ as Lord and Saviour to a costly ministry of reconciliation (2 Cor 5:18). Twenty years after the Belfast Agreement, reached on Good Friday, 10 April 1998, there remains a clear sectarian division in Northern Ireland – with largely Catholics on one side and largely Protestants on the other. This division is reflected in voting patterns for both Sinn Féin and the Democratic Unionist Party (DUP), as well as for some other political parties. The result is stalemate in the governance of Northern Ireland, this continues to alienate many people from politics and to increase acrimony in public life. A further consequence is a lack of democratic decision-making across a whole range of matters vital to the wellbeing of the people living in Northern Ireland. The Brexit process now underway, resulting from the 2016 Referendum in the United Kingdom, has compounded an already very difficult and fraught context in Ireland in respect of the principles, values and hopes embodied in the 1998 Belfast Agreement, further elaborated in the 2006 St Andrews Agreement and in the 2014 Stormont House Agreement.

Brexit, a unilateral decision by the United Kingdom, presents a very serious threat to the economic life of both Northern Ireland and the Republic of Ireland. The British-Irish Agreement that is based upon the Belfast Agreement, and which is an internationally recognised treaty, was made by 'partners in the European Union': this partnership facilitated and supported the historic Belfast Agreement as endorsed by referenda in Northern Ireland and in the Republic of Ireland. Brexit has the potential to do a great deal of further damage and harm to all the people on this island.

The legacy of the decades of violence from 1968 to 1998, and indeed later, remains unaddressed: a population of about 1.7 million has an estimated thirty per cent of people living in Northern Ireland who were directly affected – 3,720 were killed between 1969 and 2006 and about 500,000 who were bereaved, injured or suffered in other ways. The extent of the pain, trauma, anger and victimhood which lies barely under the surface of everyday life in Northern Ireland must be acknowledged: dealing with this legacy remains a core concern for those who desire a better future for everyone in the North. The hurt and trauma continues to require great pastoral concern from the churches. There is at present yet another consultation underway initiated by the Northern Ireland Office on possible structures to deal more effectively with the legacy issues of the conflict and we await decisions in respect of this initiative.

Reconciliation: a challenge for the churches

The history of Irish Christianity, in all of its denominational expressions, has resulted in a deeply embedded sectarianism, which has greatly contributed to the formation of our political identities. So, as we explore reconciliation in Ireland, we must address how the Churches have fostered sectarian attitudes since the Reformation. Sectarianism has been given a working definition as 'a complex of attitudes, beliefs, behaviours and structures in which religion is a significant component and which (i) directly, or indirectly, infringes the rights of individuals or groups and/or (ii) influences or causes situations of destructive conflict'.[2]

The Irish Church is not exceptional in a world context in being associated with violence, extremism and bigotry. In the twentieth century it was often assumed that religion would become ever more marginal to political life and to conflicts. Research, however, such as *The Future of World Religions Report*,[3] shows an increasing religious affiliation accompanied by a re-politicisation of religion: this includes a rise of religious fundamentalism across all the major world religions giving rise to conflict and violence. It is clear that religion plays many different roles in political conflicts: it may function as a proxy for ethnic, cultural or economic wrongs (real or imagined) or it may be one factor amidst a range of historic grievances, or religion may be itself a cause of conflict. Often religious factors may become so entangled with other aspects of conflict that they must also be addressed if there is to be a sustainable peace. As we struggle to shape a reconciled and shared future for all people on this island, it is important to learn from progress with reconciliation processes elsewhere and to realise that we in Ireland might also make a significant contribution to the resolution of conflicts abroad if we can successfully navigate reconciliation on this island.

In 1973 Bishop Richard Hanson stated: 'All the major denominations in Northern Ireland: Roman Catholics, Presbyterians, Church of Ireland and Methodists ... are captive Churches. They long ago sold their integrity and spiritual and intellectual independence to political ideologies in return for the massive support of the people of Northern Ireland'.[4] Marianne Elliott entitled her book, *When God Took Sides: Religion and Identity in Ireland – Unfinished History*. Former Archbishop Robin Eames entitled his book on Northern Ireland, *Unfinished Search*.[5] I suggest that the Irish churches are facing a major moment of choice as to how this 'unfinished' history and 'search' for peace concludes: they may continue as 'captive Churches' or they may be faithful to their Christ-given ministry of reconciliation. If they choose to be faithful, this will require a new, costly and radical reformation as they seek *together* to become the Church of Jesus Christ bringing the Good News to all people.

On Sunday 8 October 2017, Archbishop Eamon Martin spoke in the Church of Ireland St Patrick's Cathedral, Armagh on 'Reconciling the Reformation'. He stressed the importance of reconciliation between the Christian churches, observing that people who look upon the Church from the outside, 'particularly on this island, see a history of division and sectarianism, of intolerance, mutual recriminations, and open hostility within the Christian family'. This, he remarked, is 'a source of scandal' and he argued that we need to move 'from conflict to greater communion together bringing the joy of the Gospel into our troubled world'.

From conflict to greater communion
> Therefore, if anyone is in Christ, he is a new creation; the old has gone, the new has come! All this is from God, who reconciled us to himself through Christ and gave us the ministry of reconciliation: that God was reconciling the world to himself in Christ, not

counting men's sins against them. And he has committed to us the message of reconciliation. (2 Cor 5:17–19)

To achieve the ambition of 'greater communion', as Archbishop Martin challenges us to do, we are required to discuss the kind of theologies embraced by Irish Protestants and Irish Catholics since the Reformation. As Revd Dr Johnston McMaster has observed, Ireland has had a history and theology of violence which has never been fully analysed or acknowledged by our churches: 'We need to take violence out of the psyche, personal and collective, tackle the theological roots of sectarianism and the culture of violence. To do that we need critical analysis of the bad theology, Protestant and Catholic, which has been around for centuries, and a deconstruction of the myth of redemptive violence'.[6]

The dismal reality is that, except for some valuable individual and collective efforts, the institutional churches have not as yet undertaken this critical theological task either separately or collectively. While the conflict since 1969, and the ecumenical movement from the 1960s, pushed the Irish churches closer in instruments like the Inter-Church Meeting, this was at a price of addressing neither the causes nor the societal effects of the conflict in Ireland. What was required, and what is still the urgent task, is the full development of a common ecumenical and contextual public or political theology for the Irish situation, which will have at its centre the Gospel of Jesus Christ – the Good News of love, non-violence and human flourishing. If this task is continually reneged upon by our institutional churches, it will of course be tragic. But it will be no surprise in that case if toxic theology perpetuates divisive memories, segregated communities and potentially violent conflict.

I appreciate that in regard to 'reconciliation' there are indeed many dimensions: historical, cultural, political, socio-economic and religious. Each of these dimensions must be addressed, but we need to focus in particular on the theological and religious dimensions. *Why?* Because these are fundamental to the conflictual *mentalités* in our historical and contemporary context in Ireland. *Mentalités* denote underlying collective *frames of thought* rather than merely a set of fluctuating ideas: they tend to be deeply embedded in communities over time, as they have been in Ireland, through the process known as *confessionalisation* into either a Catholic mentality or a Protestant mentality: this has shaped popular identities as either 'British' or 'Irish'. 'Confessionalisation' refers to this long process whereby fixed identities and systems of belief emerged as separate and often bitterly divided denominations as a result of the Reformation. These 'frames of thought' have imprisoned our communities and we need to reflect on how the Gospel of reconciliation, found in Jesus Christ, may liberate us all for a shared human flourishing in the future.

It is, I believe, of great importance to understand how human flourishing ought to come to be seen as central to the Gospel and to our Christian vocation. What is central to both Scripture as a whole and to Jesus of Nazareth, is the concept of 'human flourishing'. As Miroslav Volf has observed: 'A vision of human flourishing – and the resources to realise it – is the most important contribution of the Christian faith to the common good'.[7] Our churches seem to be pre-occupied with defensive reactions to issues such as sexual abuse scandals and fending off the new consciousness in Western societies in favour of gender equality. They often appear to be overly reactive and to follow false trails to be found in a world dominated by idolatry of wealth and power. The major phenomenon of our world – the existence of great inequalities of income and wealth resulting from neo-liberalism – largely goes unchallenged, despite the efforts of Pope Francis and others to raise it, by our Irish churches. They appear to have lost a clear understanding of biblical human flourishing as central to God's reconciling and redeeming work on earth. It is urgent that we recover such an understanding and we can do it so much more effectively if we do it *together* in all our churches.

What do we mean by 'human flourishing'?
What is happiness, blessedness, *shalom*, and how does one obtain it and sustain it? The Sermon on the Mount's answer to such questions is that true human flourishing is only available through communion with the Father, through his revealed Son, Jesus, as we are empowered by the Holy Spirit: this flourishing is only experienced through faithful, heart-deep, whole-person discipleship, following Jesus's teachings, which shape how we think and behave now as disciples in God's community or kingdom. The Christian hope that flourishing will be fully experienced when God finally establishes his reign upon the earth does not devalue the true flourishing disciples experience *now* even as they experience the struggle for all to flourish-disciples still flourish through their life in Christ: 'Flourishing are the poor in spirit because the kingdom of heaven is theirs. Flourishing are the mourners because they will be comforted. Flourishing are the humble because they

will inherit the world. Flourishing are the ones hungering and thirsting for righteousness because they will be satisfied. Flourishing are the merciful because they will be given mercy. Flourishing are the pure in heart because they will see God. Flourishing are the peacemakers because they will be called the children of God. Flourishing are the ones persecuted on account of righteousness because the kingdom of heaven is theirs. Flourishing are you whenever people revile and slander and speak all kinds of evil things against you on account of me … ' (Mt 5:3–11, Pennington's translation).

The challenge to our churches is to engage in a new fundamental ecumenical reformation with a specific focus on Christian reconciliation so that we may hope for and experience true human flourishing: this requires a new emphasis on the practice of Christian discipleship for the transformation of the world. Only by such witness to true and credible reconciliation will a shared future centred upon human flourishing be practical and possible. This will be a costly sacrificial pathway – one which will dismantle much of what is sought to be maintained by our institutional churches. The current bitter battles over clericalism, misogyny and human sexuality which have divided so many of our institutional churches is symptomatic of churches that have lost their central focus on their ministry of reconciliation. Christian doctrine ought to promote human flourishing. Our churches need to set God's people free to be transformative agents of reconciliation and to equip them for whole-life discipleship in their local contexts.

The theology of Miroslav Volf

In furthering our reflections on the challenges of reconciliation, the work of Miroslav Volf, the Croatian Protestant theologian, is seminal for our context of persisting enmity between communities. His books, *Exclusion and Embrace A Theological Exploration of Identity, Otherness, and Reconciliation* (1996) and *The End of Memory. Remembering Rightly in a Violent World* (2006), are key tools for our reflections on transformative discipleship. 'Embrace' is characterised by acting with generosity toward perpetrators of evil acts and by maintaining porous boundaries and flexible identities as a mode of grace. Such 'embrace' is not opposed to 'justice', which is included as a dimension of grace extended toward wrongdoers. Maintaining 'porous boundaries' does not mean not knowing and maintaining one's own boundaries: knowing who we are in Christ is key to this and to our ability to pass judgement on evil actions or deeds. However, the concept of 'porous boundaries' is vital, as it allows us to make journeys with the 'other' in reconciliation and mutual enrichment, even as we have the confidence of who we are in Christ and recognise the image of God in the 'other'.

Volf's theology stresses God's unconditional love, justification of the ungodly, love of enemy, forgiveness: these are what we, as Christians, distinctively bring to the 'public square' and practice as a way of life. We ought to remember that, as the political philosopher, Hannah Arendt pointed out: 'The discoverer of the role of forgiveness in the realm of human affairs was Jesus of Nazareth'.[8] Forgiveness is first and foremost of benefit to those who offer it – if you find it hard to forgive, as many of us do, you probably spend a lot of time ruminating about what happened: thinking negative thoughts over and over draws us down a tunnel of negativity, worsens depression and increases anger and fear, thereby reducing empathy. Forgiveness at a personal level helps to liberate us from the debilitating power of victimhood. It enables victims to become survivors who have taken on their own power to shape their futures, instead of ceding this to the 'wrong-doers'. Forgiveness may be offered, but *reconciliation* depends upon the wrong-doer admitting their wrong deed and seizing the offer of a new relationship. Often, of course, there is glib talk about forgiveness and what it involves: forgiveness is a condition in which the sin of the past is not altered; often many of the consequences of the wrong done are not, and cannot be changed. Rather, in forgiveness a fresh act is added to those of the past, which has *the potential* to restore the broken relationship and opens the way for the one who forgives and the one who is forgiven to meet and communicate deeply with each other in the present and the future: Forgiveness heals the past, though the scars remain and many of the consequences of the sin go on, but they are taken into a fresh act of ongoing renewal and there is made possible a healing process.

The 'forgiving spirit' which Christians may embrace has been well described by Revd David Clements, a Methodist minister whose father was murdered by terrorists in 1985: 'A forgiving spirit rejects the right to retaliate. It will not consider returning evil for evil. A forgiving spirit takes the deliberate decision not to harbour hostility. The evils of the past are not forgotten, but they are not allowed to dominate the present. A forgiving spirit takes the deliberate decision to return good for evil. A forgiving spirit wants the best for those who have injured us. For the unbeliever this may be absurd, but for the Christian it is profound. It opens up the possibility of not just forgiveness but reconciliation. A forgiving spirit grows out of the knowledge of being forgiven by God in Christ. (Eph 4:32)'.

Volf emphasises the importance of truth-telling as we seek to remember the past *rightly*. He states that the proper goal of memory should be reconciliation. He claims that remembering wrongs suffered, if done rightly, will ultimately result in a positive form of 'non-remembrance' of the wrong-doing: in offering the grace and love of God, which heals relationships to such an extent that the former wrongs come to lack the emotional fuel to keep enflaming toxic relationships, they no longer come to mind in that form. Volf is, in effect, asking Christians the key question: *what kind of selves do we need to be in order to live in harmony with others?* If the Irish churches do the hard work of new theological reflection together then, I believe, they will be best equipped to foster the kind of discipleship in which Christian disciples become capable of envisioning and creating just, truthful and flourishing societies. For such disciples the imperative is the will to give ourselves to the 'other', to be prepared to welcome and be hospitable to the 'other' – this will involve a preparedness to adjust, enrich and to grow in our own identities as we make space for, and learn from, the 'other'.

The 'truth' and 'justice' that we so much seek are unavailable outside this *will to embrace* the other. 'Embrace', in the sense of full reconciliation, depends upon truth-telling and acknowledgement of wrong-doing: if our churches – who are called to be the agents of reconciliation – remain so embedded and committed to their own community's culture, which has led to such violence in the past, they will remain accomplices to any future strife. As Volf reminds us, coming to understand that other cultures are not a threat 'to the pristine purity of our cultural identity, but a potential source of its enrichment', is vital. Volf notes that indifference and unconcern for the fate of the 'other' is often more deadly than hate. The implications of this in Ireland are profound: Protestant, unionist, or British cultures and Catholic, nationalist, or Irish cultures are not inherently threats to each other, but potential sources of enrichment, creativity and global outreach from this island. Plural identities, including a European cultural identity, is the way to transcend our divided past.

We must appreciate, I believe, that no one community or group is innocent in regard to our toxic past and certainly not our churches. Can we, as Irish Christians together, accept Volf's thesis that God's reception of hostile humanity in divine reconciliation and communion is the model for how human beings should relate to each other in shaping a new and shared future?

Christian loyalty is to our Lord Jesus Christ and his mission. Our Christian obligation now is to call for truth speaking in our churches. It will not, of course, be universally popular to speak the truth as we see it, but the truth must be faced if a better future is to be shared by all on this island. It is Christians, by being prepared to face up to their toxic past, who must offer genuine hope for the future by seeking to break the bondage to the past which is preventing a flourishing future for all people on this island.

What kind of reconciliation do we seek?

The current situation demands that now be the moment of truth – it is a *Kairos* moment of crisis but it is also one of grace and opportunity. The moment of truth ought to compel each branch of the Church of Jesus Christ to analyse carefully the particular aspects of their different denominational theologies as to whether these continue to contribute to sectarian divisions which in turn underpin the divided identities and loyalties of the population of Northern Ireland. Our present *Kairos* moment calls for a response from Christians that is biblical, spiritual, pastoral and, above all, prophetic. Jesus calls his followers to 'read the signs of the times' (Mt 16:3) and to 'interpret this *Kairos* or present time' (Lk 12:56). The potential shared future is being stalled by bondage to the past. This bondage manifests itself in prevailing mind-sets. This will involve repentance for past actions or statements that contributed to divisions and bitterness.

Churches on this island have a Christ-given mission to the whole island and to the common good of the whole populations of both the Republic and Northern Ireland. This mission includes loving and serving those of other faiths and of none. The Christian mission has not been well-served by maintenance of separate missions only to each denomination's inherited flock. No church should be content to simply be reflective of nationalist or unionist political cultures, but should seek to promote the common good of all the people on the island by making a special effort to understand and empathise with the lived experience of those outside their own denominational walls. By so doing they will discover opportunities for Christian love and service together and make their witness credible.

To act prophetically each church, and our churches together, have much work to do to set a credible example of true Christian reconciliation. The churches will need to invest together in joint theological reflection to contribute, upon the basis of an agreed theological analysis of the situation, a message of genuine hope for the future as well as pathways for local church communities to follow. They will make 'hope and history rhyme' in a new and shared future.

It appears that many have hoped simply for peaceful co-existence between two segregated and politically divided communities in Northern Ireland – a sort of 'balkanisation' with two parties looking after their own side and watching what benefits the others get like hawks. This model, in operation for some years, lets the churches off the hook of their complicity in sectarian division. The model has shown that, given the current stalemate, it is not able to operate in a sustainable fashion, because it is fundamentally flawed. There has to be more to the common good if there is to be a truly shared society. The rich possibilities of *Christian reconciliation* must be explored, understood and adopted as core to the mission of Christianity in Ireland, if currently divided communities are to move beyond the flawed 'peaceful co-existence' model, which has left the churches 'captive' to their historic confessional tribes. I term this a 'moment of truth', our Irish 'Ephesian Moment': in Ephesians chapter two the radical differences between Gentiles and Jews were subsumed into a unity of diverse peoples into the 'one body', because there is only 'One Lord, One Faith, One Baptism, One God'. Only together could such different cultural and historic entities achieve their truly human flourishing in the household of God. Our churches are called now to an 'Irish Ephesian Moment' in order to be effective in their ministry of reconciliation.

Churches working together in what needs to be new ecumenical instruments, resourced to bring forward a new ecumenical and contextual public theology centred upon human flourishing and reconciliation, will be enabled to offer the peoples on this island a new and alternative narrative and a new project of human flourishing. This costly pathway will involve dismantling all the institutional and doctrinal barriers that inhibit such flourishing. It requires what some have called a 'coalition of hope' which is so badly needed for such a new project.[9]

Churches, working together, need to bring forward a rich vision of *shalom* and reconciliation that eliminates fear of 'the other' and addresses positively the sense of victimhood so pervasive in Northern Ireland. Churches need to ensure that memories are *rightly* kept with the common purpose of building in solidarity the common good; to nurture the quiet attitudinal changes at local-level – in the grass-roots and undergrowth where ultimately shifts in public opinion occur. Churches are called, I believe, to *acts of transcendence* – *to transcend* not only their culpability for the past, through repentance and lament, but also many of their doctrinal differences, which are increasingly opaque and meaningless to the populations for whom they are in *mission*, and *to transcend* their polite ecumenical contacts, too, and to re-imagine the potential for the Good News of Jesus for reconciliation which they all share.

The grim future for the Irish churches who choose to be 'captive' to their past and to their own communities is that they will be increasingly marginal to secular and pluralist society, mired in their own issues as they decay. The Irish churches still have significant collective potential – and, if they act together, they gain immense credibility for their message, enabled to exercise what may be called 'soft power' – the ability to set the agenda in ways that shape the preferences of others and which invite encounters between hitherto divided congregations. In this way they can facilitate the laity and indeed the general public to become proactive in Christian reconciliation. Imaginative, courageous and prophetic leadership is now called for in our context to change the current intransigent agendas and the historic sense of fatalism that sees Northern Ireland doomed to endless cycles of sectarian division or even further conflicts.

The Irish churches, I believe, are now challenged by the 'signs of our times' to what has been called, in another vexed context, 'living reconciliation'.[10] This does involve a costly corporate commitment by our churches to the belief that, by dying to their traditional maintenance concerns and the quest to protect their institutions, they will gain new life in God's mission as the Body of Christ in His service and ministry of reconciliation. As Archbishop Tutu said in his 1984 Nobel lecture: 'God calls us to be fellow workers with Him, so that we can extend His Kingdom of Shalom, of justice, of goodness, of compassion, of caring, of sharing, of laughter, joy, and reconciliation, so that the kingdoms of this world will become the Kingdom of our God and of His Christ, and He shall reign forever and ever. Amen'.[11]

Conclusion: living reconciliation

'Living reconciliation' is always a painful, risky, difficult journey that involves the churches becoming vulnerable: it will be most effective at local community level where some from each of the different denominations might form journeying communities gathering for purposeful discussion and seeking to discern how their response to Christian reconciliation might bear on the wounds of history, learning to live with and value difference and to celebrate diversity; serving the common good through building a common civic culture, so that all people may lead flourishing lives. We need to develop what the late Michael Hurley SJ described as a 'spirituality of reconciliation', which is about embracing relationships across boundaries and ending estrangement and bringing about friendship. On this basis *shalom* may flourish. Such a spirituality helps us to acquire a more comprehensive view of the situation as we lose our partial sight with the help of others and accept our responsibility to enable all to flourish. It ultimately involves *metanoia*, a change of heart and mind.

In conclusion, I quote Fr Hurley's words on a 'spirituality of reconciliation' from 1994: 'The ensuring dialogue is sincere and honest; it is not superficial, it is not satisfied with patching over or covering up; it goes to the roots, it is radical. Reconciliation is not cheap; it is no soft option; it does not mean peace at any price, unity at any cost. There is no reconciliation without repentance, reparation, without change, without the making of amends; there is no at-one-ment without atonement of some sort. Such a spirituality of reconciliation recognises the sacredness of the other, the primacy of love and the existence of God revealed in Christ as the one who forgives, who forgives without condoning, whose forgiveness inspires our repentance and whose example moves us to be in our turn ministers of reconciliation, forgiving those who offend us and making amends to those whom we ourselves offend'.[12]

Dr Fergus O'Ferrall was Lay Leader of the Methodist Church in Ireland, 2016–2018. He is involved in the 'coalition of hope' group that produced *A Dialogue of Hope: Critical Thinking for Critical Times*, ed. Gerry O'Hanlon SJ (2017) and he edited and contributed to *Towards a Flourishing Society* (2012). He has written books and articles on public policy and Irish history, which include *Catholic Emancipation. Daniel O'Connell and the Birth of Irish Democracy 1820–30* (1985). He is a governor of *The Irish Times*.

Notes

1   John Hewitt, 'Neither an elegy nor a manifesto' (1972), *Out of My Time: Poems 1967–1974* (Belfast: Blackstaff Press, 1974).

2   *The Report of the Working Party on Sectarianism A Discussion Document for Presentation to the Irish Inter-Church Meeting* (Irish Inter-Church Meeting, Belfast, 1993), p.8.

3   See Pew Research Centre: Populations Growth Projections, 2010–2050, updated to 2016 at www.pew.forum.org.

4   *The Guardian*, 14 September, 1973, and quoted in Maria Power, 'Providing a Prophetic Voice? Churches and Peacebuilding, 1968–2005', in Maria Power (ed.), *Building Peace in Northern Ireland* (Liverpool: Liverpool University Press, 2011).

5   Marianne Elliott, *When God Took Sides – Religion and Identity in Ireland – Unfinished History* (Oxford: Oxford University Press, 2009); Robin Eames, *Unfinished Search* (Dublin: Columba Press, 2017).

6   Johnston McMaster, *Overcoming Violence Dismantling An Irish History and Theology: An Alternative Vision*, (Dublin: Columba Press, 2012), p.8.

7   Miroslav Volf, *A Public Faith How Followers of Christ Should Serve the Common Good* (Grand Rapids, Michigan: Brazos Press, 2011) p.63. See also Volf's *Flourishing. Why We Need Religion in a Globalized World* (New Haven and London: Yale University Press, 2015) and Jonathan T Pennington, *The Sermon on the Mount and Human Flourishing A Theological Commentary* (Grand Rapids, Michigan: Baker Academic, 2017).

8   Hannah Arendt, *The Human Condition* (Chicago: University of Chicago Press, 1958), p.238.

9   On 'coalition of hope', see Gerry O'Hanlon SJ, *A Dialogue of Hope: Critical Thinking for Critical Times* (Dublin: Messenger Publications, 2017). The present writer is a part of the group which produced this book.

10 See Phil Groves and Anghared Parry Jones, *Living Reconciliation* (London: SPCK ,2014), and www.living-reconciliation.org.

11 https://www.nobelprize.org/prizes/peace/1984/tutu/acceptance-speech/

12 Michael Hurley SJ, 'Introduction', in *Reconciliation in Religion and Society* (Belfast: Institute of Irish Studies, Queen's University Belfast, 1994), pp.2–4.

Surveying Ireland after the Pope: Grounds for Cautious Optimism?

Gladys Ganiel

The contributions in *Studies'* special issue, 'Goodbye to All That? Ireland after the Pope', offer valuable insights on Francis's visit and what it reveals about the future of the Catholic Church in Ireland.[1] They share three common assumptions, two of which I wish to challenge based on my own research on the visit. The assumptions I will challenge are that the media's preoccupation with the abuse crisis was excessively negative and, as this implies, unfair; and that the visit has been largely inconsequential in the life of the Church. In contrast, my data suggest that taken as a whole, the contributors have offered an assessment of Francis's visit and the future of the Church that is bleaker than may be warranted. I will not challenge the third assumption – that there are signs of vitality still within the Church – because I also have found such signs in my previous research.

I begin with a methodological description of my research: a systematic narrative analysis of *The Irish Times* coverage of the visit between 1 May–1 September 2018, and a nationally-representative survey about the visit. I then address the two underlying assumptions in turn, explaining how my research challenges or confirms them. I conclude with brief reflections on the future of the Church. While my research challenges the somewhat pessimistic tone of the special issue, my more optimistic reading of the visit is a cautious one that leaves no room for complacency among those who wish for the Church in Ireland to *have* a future.[2]

Surveying the papal visit

A few months before Francis's visit, I was invited to contribute a chapter about Ireland to a special section on the 'Francis Effect' in *Research in the Social Scientific Study of Religion*.[3] I immediately realised that, given the attention the visit would generate, this represented a unique opportunity to attempt to measure the Francis Effect, an international phenomenon that has credited Francis with renewing Catholicism and improving the image of the

Church globally.[4] In 2017, *The Irish Times* had reported that the Irish ranked Francis as their 'favourite world leader', so it seemed Ireland was potentially fertile ground for the Francis Effect.[5]

I chose two methods for investigation. The first was a narrative analysis of *The Irish Times* coverage of the visit. I chose *The Irish Times* – second in circulation nationwide to *The Irish Independent* – because it is acknowledged as Ireland's 'newspaper of record'. I started my analysis on 1 May and continued until the weekend edition on 1 September, one week after the visit. I accessed *The Irish Times* through a searchable database in my university's library, using the term 'Pope Francis'. This turned up only a few stories that were not about the visit. Over the four-month period, there were 314 stories that mentioned Francis (21 in May, 21 in June, 16 in July, and 256 in August and on 1 September).

I identified six main themes in the stories: the abuse crisis (in Ireland and internationally), the role of women in the Church, LGBTQI people and the Church, the logistics of the visit (what the Pope was doing, how to get to events, etc.), citizens' personal perspectives on the Pope and his visit, and the Pope's personality. Abuse was the dominant theme, featuring in 46% of articles, including letters to the editor.[6] I even went so far as to claim that 'the national conversation became dominated by the issue of abuse – so much so that the visit seemed to have become an unofficial referendum on the papal response to abuse'.[7] But this conclusion is not quite the same as implying that the media's coverage of abuse was excessive or unfair, as explored below.

My second method was a nationally-representative survey designed to evaluate evidence of a Francis Effect.[8] I considered the Francis Effect measurable in terms of changes in people's perspectives on the Church or changes in their religious practice since Francis became pope and since Francis's visit. I asked questions about changes in perspectives on the Church and about specific religious practices. Because the coverage around the visit had focused so much on abuse, I also asked about Francis's handling of abuse during the visit and if abuse had been a reason for not attending events. Some of these questions echoed those of an opinion poll carried out by *The Irish Times* the day after the visit. My questions were included in a regular, monthly omnibus survey conducted by Amarach, mid-to-late September 2018. Amarach considers questions about religion 'sensitive', so people could opt-out of my questions. Amarach's sample was 840, with quotas set on gender, age, social class and region, aligning with the national population in the Republic; Northern Ireland was not included. The survey was completed online, a valid approach given the reach of the internet in Ireland.

Media coverage

Tom Inglis has argued that the media has played a central role in the Church's decline, first by exposing the public to alternative, secular and materialistic lifestyles; and second, through its coverage of the abuse scandals.[9] More than three decades after the first edition of *Moral Monopoly,* Susie Donnelly and Inglis wrote that the media had 'replaced the Catholic Church as the social conscience and moral guardian of Irish society'.[10] Moreover, they claimed that the media depicted the Church 'as evil' and 'as a public enemy'.[11]

The editorial that introduced the special issue of *Studies* asserted a similar relationship between Church and media. It referred to the media's 'framing' of the visit in terms of the abuse crisis, arguing that, 'Such framing ... can distort what, in fact, is a much longer, much more complex history and it is only fair to say that it also distorted interpretations of and responses to the papal visit, before, during and after'.[12] The most thorough and compelling treatment of the media was Andrew McMahon's contribution, which lamented a prevailing media 'groupthink'. He opened by citing a *Sunday Times* article from the weekend after the visit in which a writer referred to a 'consensus' that the pope 'did not go far enough in terms of outlining the steps he intends to take to ensure that abuse is eradicated from the Church'. McMahon then observed that the article did not 'offer specific evidence in support of so significant a conclusion'.[13] While he is right to question unsubstantiated claims, an opinion poll published in *The Irish Times* on 28 August and my own survey confirm that the most popular opinion among people in Ireland was indeed that the Pope had not gone far enough. *The Irish Times* poll reported 55% of respondents said Francis had not gone far enough, with 31% saying he had gone far enough, and 14% with no opinion. I repeated *The Irish Times* question in my own survey, finding that 48% indicated he had not gone far enough, 30% said he had gone far enough, and 22% had no opinion.[14] While it may be a stretch to say that either 55% or 48% is a 'consensus', in both studies it was the most popular opinion. However, in my survey there was a significant difference among practising Catholics (defined as those who go to religious services at least once per month): 50% said Francis had gone far enough, while just 28% said he had not.

McMahon also linked *The Irish Times* coverage of the Pennsylvania

Grand Jury report on clerical child abuse, which broke less than two weeks before Francis was due to arrive, with its interview with Ian Elliott, the former head of the Irish Church's National Board for Safeguarding Children. The interview was conducted during the Pennsylvania coverage, and Elliott was critical of the Church's safeguarding practices. McMahon claimed this was 'an important piece of strategy by *The Irish Times* ... guaranteed to undermine, at a critical moment, whatever public confidence the Irish Church had garnered in this area'.[15] But given his former position, Elliott is a reasonable choice for an interview; to attribute his inclusion as a malign strategising against the Church may be going too far. Moreover, McMahon referred to a 'panic' about abuse in the press as Francis' visit drew nearer.[16] But he didn't mention that the Vatican's refusal to confirm whether Francis would meet any survivors at all until only a few days before the visit had become a story in and of itself, which may have fed this 'panic' just as much as or more than Elliott's interview.

Further, on several occasions *The Irish Times* pointed out that Dublin archbishop Diarmuid Martin was internationally respected for his work on safeguarding. Patsy McGarry even presented Martin as a sort of super-hero who Francis could put to good use in reforming the Church:[17] 'So what would you do if you were Pope Francis? Very simple. I'd bring Archbishop Diarmuid Martin back to Rome with me. I'd put him in charge of a new tribunal at the Vatican whose sole brief would be to hold bishops and religious superiors to account for covering up/facilitating the abuse of children and vulnerable people. I'd give him the power to remove the truly errant ones among them from office. Then I'd sit back and watch with pleasure as he kicked some very deserving ass'.

The Irish Times also included stories about citizens' personal perspectives on Francis, and the Pope's personality, which presented more positive images of the Church. These stories may have become lost alongside the emphasis on abuse; indeed, one could read the special issue without realising that such coverage existed. My analysis of *The Irish Times* coverage recognises that more positive perspectives were not entirely absent and its coverage was somewhat more nuanced than the special issue implies. At the same time, while my analysis was systematic, it was limited: I examined the coverage of just one print media outlet. I am not aware of any studies that have systematically analysed a wide range of media coverage of the visit.

It may be the case that the Irish media have been more critical of the

Church than of the state when it comes to handling the abuse crisis. That is my personal impression, albeit one I cannot back up with systematic data. So to some degree I sympathise with the assumptions about the media in the special issue. But to make such a claim with confidence would require systematic analysis of widespread media coverage of Church and state both during the visit and over many years. In the absence of such research, the Church should heed Gerry O'Hanlon's advice in the special issue: a 'contrite' Church 'should not over-complain (considering its own considerable guilt)'.[18] Indeed, in an Irish context, where many survivors still feel abuse has not been adequately addressed, it would have been unthinkable for the media *not* to focus on this issue when the Pope was in town.

Finally, we must remember that the failure of the Church to adequately address abuse remains a pressing problem worldwide. If this were not the case, Francis would not have called a special summit on abuse in February 2019, summoning to Rome the president of every Catholic bishops' conference in the world, as well as religious superiors. Abuse in the Church was and is a crime; in the worst cases, it could be argued that the Church committed widespread human rights violations, with the support or acquiescence of the state. Without the hard work of investigative journalists in many countries over the years, that abuse might remain hidden.

Francis's visit has been inconsequential
Some quotes from the special issue will suffice to illustrate the assumption that Francis's visit has been inconsequential in the life of the Church (or the wider country). Michael Kirwan wrote: 'Memorable as it was, it has left no apparent disturbance or alteration of the trajectory we are getting used to: that Ireland is a secularising, if not already secularised, society, in which Christian faith is increasingly marginal'.[19] Stephen Collins concluded: 'There is a general consensus that the visit of Pope Francis to Ireland last summer failed to make any serious impact on the country'.[20] Brendan Hoban was perhaps most dramatic:[21] 'The jury is out on whether the Irish Catholic Church has a discernible future, apart from a ceremonial presence on the official side lines of Irish life or a refuge for those ill at ease with the modern world. Because its presence as such, apart from being a convenient scape-goat for the ills of Irish society, has virtually disappeared in the media, in public debate, in modern Irish writing, in the lives of the young'.

It is certainly true that the Church is not the social and political force it once was, but to claim it has 'virtually disappeared' is going too far. A wide range of sociological research has confirmed that Ireland remains one of the most religious countries in Europe.[22] And although Breda O'Brien cautions that 'although those statistics are high by European standards, the faith is being hollowed out from within in a way that the statistics fail to reveal',[23] I am not convinced that the situation is quite as extreme as suggested, or the visit as inconsequential as claimed. Bearing in mind O'Brien's caution about statistics, my survey shows that people's perceptions and experiences of the visit were not solely dominated by abuse, and that there is some evidence for a modest 'Francis Effect' in Ireland, especially among practising Catholics and those under age thirty-five. Below, I pay particular attention to 18–24-year olds, because of their obvious importance if the Church is to have a future.[24]

In the survey, 64% of respondents identified as Catholic – 14% lower than the 78% recorded on the 2016 Census. The next largest category was 'no religion' at 19% – higher than the 10% on the census. This figure rose to 29% among 18–24-year olds. It is possible that the difference between the figures on religious identification on the census and the survey is because people of 'no religion' were more likely to opt to complete the survey, perhaps to express their dissatisfaction with religion.

People were asked if they attended events associated with the visit, and their reasons why or why not. Twenty per cent of all respondents attended events. Both practising Catholics (37%) and 18-24-year olds (29%) were more likely to attend events than the general population.[25] For the general population, the most popular reasons for attending were 'to be part of a big national event' (51%), 'to express my faith' (47%) and as a guardian or carer (16%).[26] Among practising Catholics the figures were 'to express my faith (63%), 'to be part of a big national event' (51%) and as a guardian or carer (10%). The 18–24-year olds were the age group most likely to attend 'to express my faith' at 65%; 55% attended to be part of a big national event, and 23% as a guardian or carer. This question can be compared to one asked by *The Irish Times,* where the overall figures on reasons for attending were 59% (national event), 66% (express faith) and 18% (guardian/carer). The biggest difference between the surveys was among those attending to 'express faith' – it was 19% higher in *The Irish Times* poll. This may be due to the timings of the surveys. People who have recently attended an event, in some cases less than twenty-four hours previously, may still feel uplifted by it, and may have been more likely to cite faith as a factor. But I cannot claim this explanation is conclusive.

Of the 80% who did not attend events, 51% did not because 'I was not interested' and 30% did not because 'I disagree with how the Catholic Church has handled child sex abuse'. For practising Catholics, the top reason they did not attend was because the travel/walk was too difficult (39%), followed by lack of interest (22%) and disagreement with how the Church has handled abuse (18%). Among those with 'no religion', 73% were not interested and 40% disagreed with the handling of abuse. For 18–24-year olds, 64% did not attend because they were not interested and 32% because they disagreed with how the Church had handled abuse.[27] So for everyone except practising Catholics, indifference seems to have trumped anger about abuse as a reason for not attending – although abuse is still the next most significant factor (Table 1).

Table 1: Reasons for not attending an event (% respondents)

I did not attend because:	All N = 676	Practising Catholics N=129	Other Catholics N=301	Non-Catholics, N=85	No Religion, N=153	18-24 year-olds N=53
I was not interested	51	22	52	52	73	64
I disagree with how the Catholic Church has handled child sex abuse	30	18	31	27	40	32
The travel/walk to the venue was too difficult	17	39	17	9	2	11
I disagree with the teachings of the Catholic Church	14	2	9	18	34	25
I was not in favour of the Pope's visit	12	2	10	15	24	23

Continued over

I disagree with how Pope Francis is leading the Catholic Church	7	2	4	13	15	9
I was unable to get a ticket to the event	4	5	4	6	1	6
I was at work/ out of the country	3	8	3	4	1	5
I attended an event protesting Pope Francis' visit instead	1	0	1	1	2	3
The weather was poor even though I had a ticket	1	1	1	1	1	0

I gauged people's perceptions of the visit by asking if they agreed or disagreed with seven statements about it (Table 2). The statement about Francis' handling of abuse has been discussed above. Again, practising Catholics differed from everyone else in that they reported much more positive perceptions about the visit; however, 18–24-year olds were in line with the general population on these questions. For example, when asked whether the visit was 'a healing time for victims and survivors of clerical sex abuse', overall 36% disagreed and 31% agreed; when asked whether it was 'a healing time for LGBTQI people and their families', 40% disagreed and 23% agreed. But among practising Catholics, 54% agreed that it was a healing time for victims and survivors (23% disagreed); and 37% agreed it was a healing time for LGBTQI people (21% disagreed). When asked if the visit was 'good for Ireland as a nation', 48% agreed, with just 26% disagreeing. A further 50% agreed that the visit 'was good for the Catholic Church in Ireland', with just 21% disagreeing. Almost one-in-four, 24%, agreed that the visit 'will revive faith in Ireland'. Practising Catholics differed again: 75% thought the visit was good for Ireland and 73% thought it was good for the Church; 47% thought it would revive faith. It is worth repeating that a full 50% of the general population and 73% of practising Catholics thought the visit was good for the Church. If the situation of the Church in Ireland was/is in any way as dire as some writers in the special issue of *Studies* suggested, these are quite astounding numbers. (However, it must be admitted that some respondents could have interpreted the question to mean that it was 'good' that the Church was held to account for abuse during the visit, rather than that it was 'good' for faith or the public image of the Church, or any other way this statement could be interpreted). Likewise, it is quite astounding that 24% of the general population thought the visit would revive faith. This is not an insignificant minority; nor is the 47% of practising Catholics who thought the visit would revive faith.

Table 2: Perceptions of Francis' Visit (% respondents) [28]

	Disagree	Agree	Neither/ nor	No opinion
It was good for Ireland as a nation, Overall, N=840	26	48	23	3
It was good for Ireland as a nation, Practising Catholics, N=206	8	75	16	*
It was good for Ireland as a nation, 18-24 years old, N=75	33	40	21	4
It was good for the Catholic Church in Ireland, Overall, N=840	21	50	26	3
It was good for the Catholic Church in Ireland, Practising Catholics, N=206	7	73	18	1
It was good for the Catholic Church in Ireland, 18-24 years old, N=75	24	47	25	5
The Pope went far enough during his visit to address child sex abuse in the Catholic Church, Overall, N=840	48	30	19	3
The Pope went far enough during his visit to address child sex abuse in the Catholic Church, Practising Catholics, N=206	28	50	21	2

Continued over

The Pope went far enough during his visit to address child sex abuse in the Catholic Church, 18-24 years old, N=75	45	34	15	6
It was a healing time for victims and survivors of clerical sex abuse, Overall, N=840	36	31	21	3
It was a healing time for victims and survivors of clerical sex abuse, Practising Catholics, N=206	23	54	21	2
It was a healing time for victims and survivors of clerical sex abuse, 18-24 years old, N=75	50	27	20	3
It was a healing time for LGBTQI people and their families, Overall, N=840	40	23	32	5
It was a healing time for LGBTQI people and their families, Practising Catholics, N=206	21	37	37	6
It was a healing time for LGBTQI people and their families, 18-24 years old, N=75	53	21	20	4
It will revive faith in Ireland, Overall, N=840	46	24	28	2
It will revive faith in Ireland, Practising Catholics, N=206	20	47	32	*
It will revive faith in Ireland, 18-24 years old, N=75	51	25	23	1
It was as important as the visit of Pope John Paul II in 1979, Overall, N=840	45	32	19	4
It was as important as the visit of Pope John Paul II in 1979, Practising Catholics , N=206	29	54	16	1
It was as important as the visit of Pope John Paul II in 1979, 18-24 years old, N=75	45	31	13	9

Four of the questions were designed to gauge a Francis Effect. First, 'Has your opinion of the Catholic Church changed since Francis became Pope in 2013?' There was no change for 66% of the general population, although 22% said that their opinion had become more favourable. Among practising Catholics, 39% said their opinion had become more favourable, with 57% unchanged. Among those 18–24, 27% were more favourable and 54% were unchanged. The 25–34 age group was the only one more changeable than the 18–24, with 32% more favourable and 53% unchanged. In *The Irish Times* poll, a similar question revealed that, overall, 38% had a more positive view of the Church with Francis as Pope (51% of practising Catholics), with no change among 58% (47% of practising Catholics). Second, 'Has your opinion of the Catholic Church changed since Pope Francis visited Ireland?' Seventy-four per cent (66% of practising Catholics and 64% of 18–24-year olds) said their opinion was unchanged; the figure was 80% unchanged in a similar question on *The Irish Times* poll. Sixteen per cent (30% of practising Catholics and 19% of 18–24-year olds) indicated that their opinion of the Church had become more favourable since the visit; 11% (4% of practising Catholics and 17% of 18–24-year olds) indicated their opinion had become less favourable. Again the 25–34 age group was the only one more changeable than the 18–24, with 62% unchanged, 19% more favourable and 12% less favourable. There are not comparable more/less favourable figures for *The Irish Times* poll.

The other two Francis Effect questions addressed changes in religious practice: 'Has your religious practice changed as a result of Francis becoming Pope in 2013?' and 'Do you anticipate that your religious practice will change as a result of Pope Francis visiting Ireland?' For both questions, people were given a range of options and could tick all that applied. Overall, most people indicated that their practice had not changed (63%) and would not change (63%) – figures similar to practising Catholics (64% since Francis became Pope, and 62% after the visit). However, younger people were more likely to report changes in practice: just 47% of 25–34-year olds and 46% of 18–24-year olds said there were no changes. For practising Catholics, the top three ways in which religious practice had changed or would change (ranging from 16 to 12%) were praying more often, being more kind and merciful to family and friends, and attending religious services more often. Francis's visit also prompted 8% of practising Catholics to say they would give more of their time and money to helping the poor, and 7% to go to confession more often. Among the two youngest age brackets, the most popular change was praying more often (15% of 25–34-year olds and 12% of 18–24-year olds). People in these age brackets also anticipated going to religious services more often (10% in both age brackets versus 5% overall) and going to confession more often (10% of 18–24-year olds and 6% of 25–34-year olds versus 3% overall).

To summarise and repeat a few figures, a sizeable minority of the general population (22%), practising Catholics (39%), and 18–24-year olds (27%) have a more favourable view of the Church since Francis became pope. There also have been changes in religious practices among a minority, in a direction that could be described as more devotional, especially among practising Catholics and people under thirty-five. People under thirty-five were much more likely to report that their practices had changed or would change as a result of Francis becoming pope or his visit. To some extent, this simply reflects the expected volatility of youth; people may still be trying out religious practices before settling into lifelong patterns – or not practising religion at all, as indicated by 24% of 18–24-year olds and 15% of 25–34-year olds. I cannot put a figure on what percentage of people would need to have changed their views or practices for a Francis Effect to be declared valid in Ireland. But all things considered, the survey results point to at least a partial Francis Effect despite dissatisfaction with the handling of abuse (and LGBTQI issues), and to an openness among the younger generation to change their views of the Church (for better or for worse) and to change their religious practices.

Concluding reflections

In his contribution to the special issue of *Studies*, Collins wrote: 'Only time will tell whether Ireland after the Pope will provide an opportunity for Church renewal but, if the right lessons are learned, it could mark a turning point'.[29] This was just one of the strands of optimism scattered throughout the articles, which overall painted a bleaker picture of the Church's future.

While the abuse crisis dominated media coverage, this reflected concerns – in Ireland and globally – that the Church has not done enough to address abuse and to ensure that it does not happen again. One of the lessons that needs to be learned is that the Church must be more just and consistent in its approach to abuse, including cooperating with civil authorities around the world. The Church also must communicate more effectively about how it is addressing abuse, especially with the media. At the same time, it is important to recognise the perception, articulated in the special issue of *Studies*, that media coverage of the Church was and is excessively hostile or unfair. Last year, when I presented the initial findings of my papal visit research to a gathering of priests, they were surprised that abuse featured in 'only' 46% of *The Irish Times* stories. Many people in the Church feel they are under attack in the media, and this perception must surely impact on their own identities and sense of self, and in the case of clergy, their ability to minister with confidence among the people. Feelings of beleaguerment may be coupled with a real and felt powerlessness to respond to the abuse crisis in their everyday lives and ministry.

At the same time, my survey revealed that sizeable minorities of the general population, and especially practising Catholics and people under thirty-five, are open to a more favourable view of the Church, and more engagement with it through changing their religious practices, than might have been expected.[30] While the nature of survey research militates against evaluating the depth of such changes towards devotion, such figures may give cause for a more cautious optimism among those who wish for the Church in Ireland to *have* a future. It also may be that I overstated the special issue contributors' pessimism; after all, many of them listed small-scale, local initiatives that demonstrated religious vitality. I also have found such signs in previous research.[31]

But my more optimistic reading of the papal visit is a cautious one. After all, much dissatisfaction with abuse remains, the under-thirty-five age brackets are always more prone to change, and the Francis Effect is itself a rather ephemeral concept. The Francis Effect's positive perceptions about the Church are no substitute for the real and substantial changes in Church structures that are required for more lasting change, as Gerry O'Hanlon's urgent writings about the need for synodal Church have reminded us.[32] It will take a long work of passion and creativity for new initiatives to capture the wider imagination, both inside the Church and without it. The window of opportunity for the Church in Ireland to capitalise on relative levels of positivity and openness may be small, and may close quickly without urgent and immediate action.

Gladys Ganiel is a sociologist at Queen's University Belfast. Her latest book, *Unity Pilgrim: The Life of Fr Gerry Reynolds CSsR*, a popular biography of a peacemaking priest at Belfast's Clonard Monastery, was published by Redemptorist Communications in 2019.

Notes

1 *Studies* CVIII, 430 (2019).
2 I wish to thank Gerry O'Hanlon and Vincent O'Sullivan for helpful comments on this research. I remain responsible for my interpretations and errors.
3 Gladys Ganiel, 'Negating the Francis Effect?: The Effect of the Abuse Crisis in Ireland', in Giuseppe Giordan (ed.), *Research in the Social Scientific Study of Religion*, vol. 29, special edition on the Francis Effect (Leiden: Brill, 2019 forthcoming).
4 Sarah Eekhoff Zylstra, 'Pew: No Pope Francis 'Effect' among US Christians', *Christianity Today*, 2018,
5 Michael O'Regan, 'Pope Francis is Ireland's Favourite World Leader', *The Irish Times*, 29 December 2017.
6 Most stories included multiple themes.
7 Ganiel, 'Negating the Francis Effect?'
8 Gladys Ganiel, 'Surveying the Papal Visit to Ireland: A Francis Effect?', Queen's Policy Engagement Paper 2, October 2018, http://qpol.qub.ac.uk/wp-content/uploads/2018/10/Gladys-Ganiel-Paper-on-Pope-Francis.pdf
9 Tom Inglis, *Moral Monopoly: The Rise and Fall of the Catholic Church in Modern Ireland, 2nd Ed.* (Dublin: UCD Press, 1998). The first edition was published in 1987, before the extent of the abuse scandals became known.
10 Susie Donnelly and Tom Inglis, 'The Media and the Catholic Church in Ireland: Reporting Clerical Child Sexual Abuse', *Journal of Contemporary Religion*, 25(1), 2010, 1.
11 Donnelly and Inglis, 'The Media and Catholic Church in Ireland', 14.
12 'Editorial', *Studies* CVIII, 430 (2019), 118.
13 Andrew McMahon, ' "New" Ireland and Pope Francis', *Studies* CVIII, 430 (2019), 138.
14 Pat Leahy, 'Majority in Poll Say Pope Failed to do Enough on Abuse During Visit', *The Irish Times*, 28 August 2018.
15 McMahon, '"New Ireland" and Pope Francis', 142.
16 McMahon, '"New Ireland" and Pope Francis', 142.
17 Pasty McGarry, 'Being Pope these Days Means Forever having to Say You're Sorry', *The Irish Times*, 21 August 2018.
18 Gerry O'Hanlon SJ, 'After the Pope – the Catholic Church in Ireland', *Studies* CVIII, 430 (2019), 135.
19 Michael Kirwan SJ, 'An Abrahamic Journey: Ireland, Faith and the Papal Visit', *Studies* CVIII, 430 (2019), 162.
20 Stephen Collins, 'After the Visit: Re-Learning our Past', *Studies* CVIII, 430 (2019), 195.
21 Brendan Hoban, 'Another Beginning?' *Studies* CVIII, 430 (2019), 157.
22 For a few examples, see Pew Research Center, 'Being Christian in Western Europe', 2018; Stephen Bullivant, 'Europe's Young Adults and Religion', 2018, available at https://www.stmarys.ac.uk/research/centres/benedict-xvi/docs/2018-mar-europe-

young-people-report-eng.pdf; Kristen Andersen, 'Irish Secularization and Religious Identities: Evidence of an Emerging New Catholic Habitus', *Social Compass* 57(1), 2010, 15–39.

23 Breda O'Brien, 'Young People and the Future of the Irish Church', *Studies* 108(430), Summer 2019, 187.

24 See especially O'Brien, 'Young People and the Future of the Irish Church'.

25 Bear in mind that this age category contains 29% of people who identify as 'no religion'.

26 The most likely age group to attend events was 25–34, at 38%.

27 Respondents could choose more than one option.

28 The categories Disagree and Agree contain and combine the qualifiers 'slightly' and 'strongly'.

29 Collins, 'After the Visit', 202.

30 The overall sample of 840 included 75 age 18–24 and 147 aged 25–34, in line with national proportions. So caution also must be used when interpreting samples of 75 and 147. At the same time, other research indicates that Ireland's young people rank among the most religious in Europe: see Stephen Bullivant, *Europe's Young Adults and Religion: Findings from the European Social Survey* (2014–16) to inform the Synod of Bishops' (London: Benedict XVI Centre for Religion and Society, 2018).

31 Gladys Ganiel, *Transforming Post-Catholic Ireland: Religious Practice in Late Modernity* (Oxford: Oxford University Press, 2019).

32 Gerry O'Hanlon, *The Quiet Revolution of Pope Francis: A Synodal Catholic Church in Ireland?* (Dublin: Messenger Publications, 2018).

Irish Politics and Brexit Failure

William Kingston

A 'no-deal' Brexit obviously means a hard border in Ireland, and with the election of Prime Minister Boris Johnson, the danger of it has greatly increased. Irish policy-makers consequently need to learn and reflect on how much they contributed to her failure. An over-playing of the Irish hand seriously hampered the British negotiating stance.

The UK, in fact, has little need to put up a barrier on the border, since any future imports from the EU are likely to be more expensive than those from elsewhere, but Brussels would *have* to have one. Once cheaper food starts to be imported into Britain, there will be money to be made from moving it into the EU. Only a hard EU border *on the Irish side* can physically stop this, and French farmers, not to speak of our own, would insist on it, and instantly.

Instead of seeking to tie Britain's hands in the negotiations, therefore, Irish policy should have been to do everything possible to help them get the best possible deal. Unfortunately, what happened illustrates yet again that those who negotiate for us lack awareness of one of the most crucial components of all deal-making, and also do not seem to be able to learn from their failures.

The most important key to successful negotiation is to ensure that the other party also profits from the outcome. This means never pushing whatever strength one may have to the limit. Irish policy-makers instead appear to use their power in any situation with its maximum force.

As Noel Dorr showed in his recent book, *Sunningdale: the Search for Peace in Northern Ireland*, we have been here before in the Sunningdale Agreement. There were two components in this: power-sharing and the 'Irish dimension'. Power-sharing was introduced and had started to work. However, given the violent history to which it was a partial response, it needed a long period to bed in. There was no urgent need to invoke the Irish dimension, but the Agreement had put the power to do this into the hands of Liam Cosgrave's government, which used it and brought the roof in. The result was the Ulster Workers' strike, the destruction of Brian Faulkner's brand of moderate Unionism, the irresistible rise of Ian Paisley and the DUP, and many more years of bloodshed.

In the same way, when the British electorate voted for Brexit, the Irish government had power related to the negotiations because of its land border with the UK and the goodwill of EU States and especially of Britain. It has been altogether overlooked that at no stage did London even threaten to play its strongest card against us, which is the Common Travel Area. Again, the Irish power was used to the limit, without understanding of the possible consequences, in respect of the *preconditions* for negotiating future terms of trading between the parties.

Once it became known that the EU intended to lay down preconditions before trade matters could be discussed, it was in this country's interest to keep the border issue out of them, so as to push dealing with it into the substantive phase. Such Irish influence as there was should have been used to limit preconditions to the two that were quite capable of being dealt with without any reference to trade. These are the position of citizens from the EU who are living in the UK, and vice versa, and the amount of alimony to be paid by Britain in the divorce proceedings.

Instead, as with Sunningdale, the power in the hands of the Irish government was used to the limit, to make a border without checks a third precondition. This certainly did not happen on the initiative of the EU – there was no reason why they should think it up. Incorporating the Irish demand that Britain give assurances about the border in advance was then presented as a triumph, when in fact it was a diplomatic failure. Lecturing the British that 'the onus is on them to deliver a seamless border' and enabling M. Barnier to say that 'Those who want Brexit must come up with solutions', compounded this error. Any such guarantee – if indeed one were possible at all – should only have been part of whatever trade deal eventually emerged.

Satisfying this precondition was intrinsically impossible, therefore, the Irish insistence on it led to the 'backstop' on which Mrs May's deal with the EU foundered. This has now greatly increased the danger of Britain having to leave the EU without any deal at all – the worst possible outcome for Ireland. If this does happen, much of the blame must be laid on those who were responsible for making Irish concerns the third precondition.

This would be an even greater failure than that of the destruction of the Sunningdale Agreement, and it would have been caused by the same flaw in negotiating ability. Just how much greater will only become clear when the nature of the EU's external border with the UK is finally settled.

To call attention to the Irish contribution is not in any way to diminish Mrs

May's own mistakes, which began with her hasty 'Brexit is Brexit', when, to adapt Burke's famous phrase, she 'betrayed instead of serving the electorate, by sacrificing her judgement to its opinion'.

A referendum can only identify what people would like to have happen in their ideal world, which is why direct democracy cannot work. The value of a representative system is that it can articulate for voters how far, and in what ways, these wishes can be realised in the real world, full as it is of interests, antagonisms and need for compromise. The incompatibility of the two systems is perfectly illustrated by Mrs May's unstinting but vain attempts to put flesh on an aspiration of a majority of the British electorate in a context of realities that could not accommodate it.

It is possible that we could be saved from the UK crashing out of the EU at the end of October by a Commons vote to revoke Article 50 if reluctant Tories see that as the only alternative to a general election. This would also free the new EU administration from having to claim that the Barnier–May Agreement is set in stone. Nevertheless, the danger remains great.

This country will again have some influence on the EU's stance, but this time we should tread softly because we tread on English dreams, dreams we have helped turn into a nightmare.

William Kingston is in the TCD Business School and the author of *Interrogating Irish Policies.*

Autonomy within the European Union: A Relational Perspective

Ray and Maurice Kinsella

Introduction

The European Union (EU) has, over the last decade, been scarred – and indeed its viability called into question – by a succession of interrelated crises. This period of instability dates, more or less, from the European banking crisis, including the resultant economic and socio-political instability across the eurozone and the wider EU. But the epicentre of what can best be described as a truly *existential* crisis goes much deeper – from economic inequality and the near eclipse of Social Europe, to a yawning democratic deficit that has created a widespread sense of disenchantment and alienation from the European Project (as has been given expression in the ongoing Brexit debacle). The resultant tensions have often been rendered, imperfectly, as 'populism'.

At the heart of these strains is the pressure between two tectonic forces, the perception of an increasingly hegemonistic EU and the aspiration to recover iteratively eroded national autonomy. This is a consistent theme that has emerged from a succession of national elections across the EU. It is real and authentic and the single greatest priority of the new European Commission and parliament is to engage reflectively with this phenomenon, beginning with a renewed understanding of autonomy. We explore this pivotally important issue in this paper.

Autonomy, as a form of self-law (*auto-nomos*), can be conceptually excavated in two distinct but related ways. Firstly, from a *philosophical* perspective, autonomy is a concept that contributes towards our understanding of the socio-political ontology of nations and their attendant normative and legislative status. Secondly, from a *practical* perspective, it is the iteratively realised capacity that encompasses taking ownership not just of specific decisions and actions, but over a broader national narrative: to govern in accordance with justifications and motivations that are authentically the nation's own, rather than the product of coercive forces.[1] To address the question, 'What path do we wish to carve out for ourselves as a nation?', therefore first necessitates answering, even to a limited degree,'*who are we as a nation?*' Autonomy is, in this instance, the recognition and realisation of this insight – to progressively *become oneself amongst others* and, aligned with this, to construct a national narrative that is both authentic and meaningful.

In section one, we put forward a provisional model of autonomy as 'becoming oneself amongst others'; in particular focusing on its relational-rootedness and the significance that this has within the context of EU relations. In section two, we reflect on the extent to which imposed austerity – which is expressed in 'Troikanomics' – is indicative of a chronic undermining of EU member nations' autonomy. In section three we develop this analysis by exploring how Troikanomics has subverted a set of *specific* autonomous capacities possessed by EU member nations. Looking to the future, a challenge for the EU is the extent to which it is prepared to critique the nature and purpose of intra-EU relationships, to learn lessons from Troikanomics, and to appreciate national autonomy's relational-rootedness.[2]

Autonomy: a relationally fostered capacity
National autonomy is the relational capacity to move towards a sense of clarity and coherence in *who one is* as a nation, and to express this understanding within one's national pursuits. This process of 'becoming oneself among others' emerges through the coalescence of three autonomous capacities: self-governance, self-determination and self-affirmation. *Self-governance* is a nation's capacity to critically engage with, and respond to, the range of characteristics that constitute its 'domestic identity'. *Self-determination* is a nation's capacity to critically engage with, and respond to, the range of characteristics comprising its transnational environment. *Self-affirmation* is a nation's capacity to trust in its own legitimacy as an autonomous entity – encompassing its right to affirm and be answerable for 'who they are' amidst a multitude of other nations.[3]

Every country believes that they have a claim on autonomy – that their capacity to exercise ownership over their trajectory is a *right* that should be upheld in the treaties, policies and provisions that form and foster transnational relationships. This quest for autonomy serves as a motivational force, which we find evidence of in the manifestos of politicians, in democratic representativeness, in the carving out of economic niches, in the symbolism of flags and national anthems, in the companionship that comes after national tragedy and in the pride that comes with national success. Each of these is, in its own way, an expression of this impetus towards not just taking ownership over one's national identity, but taking ownership over the *nation one wishes to become.*

'Relational' perspectives assert that autonomous agency is 'embedded' i.e. a capacity that is nurtured (or indeed, as is so often the case, *impeded*) through ongoing relationships.[4] The complex communal tapestry within which members of the EU are interwoven can therefore both enable and obstruct them in reaching more optimal levels of functioning. In a positive context, autonomy is progressively realised *amongst* others, as opposed to being in a state of radical extrication *from* others. Thus, nations' geopolitical and economic interactions are not simply 'external' events to be navigated, but are internalisable and imbue consequences that reverberate throughout the political, economic, and social fabric of the nation itself.

Given that international communities, such as the EU, consistently struggle to stave off internal conflict (through means such as cooperation, compromise, consolidation and also, it must be said, enforcement), national autonomy should not be seen as a realistic aspiration in any *'radical'* sense. Instead, it is best achieved through negotiating the opportunities and constraints that communal participation brings with it – making the most of one's place in the community. While autonomy may be a worthy 'ideal' to strive towards, the *reality* of autonomy can therefore only be accomplished in a 'non-ideal' sense – always balanced between forces that nations are capable of maintaining control of and those that are beyond their grasp.[5] Therefore, while the full and unimpeded expression of nations' autonomy is not possible, the EU *should still* strive to create an environment within which members' autonomous capacities can progressively be more fully recognised and realised.

Relational perspectives distinguish between autonomy and substantive independence so as to dispel the belief that participation in transnational relationships (be they bilateral or multilateral) necessitates the *sacrifice* of autonomy. The crux of this perspective is that a hard-line 'trade-off' between these two *seeming* polarities fails to do justice to the centrality of dialogue. The oft-idealised goal of substantive independence is, in this reading, increasingly unworkable and counter to the growing interconnectivity between nations within communities such as the EU –

as is apparent in trade relationships and labour mobility.

It would appear, certainly, that the forces of supranational federalism and globalisation (as expressed through communications technologies and the pervasive influence of multinational corporates) have ushered in a paradigm shift in how we understand transnational interconnectedness. Conventional wisdom asserts that globalisation makes national autonomy redundant – either as an achievement or an aspiration.[6] This is, however, a clever piece of sophistry and fails to acknowledge the role that autonomy continues to play in mediating relationships, as well as in informing their *very real* legal/normative underpinnings. It is a loaded argument that leeches away the proper responsibilities of national governments without safeguarding the scope for vindicating principles that draw on the internal capacities of nations.

The radically important point here is that *being-in-community* should not displace the inherent right that nations have to exercise their autonomy, nor their capacity to do so. Rather, it places on their communities the responsibility to be attentive to the fostering of this ability and the upholding of this right, not as a rhetorical device but as something embedded in policies and mind- sets and continually critiqued. Autonomy does not call for 'external' political/economic relations to be rejected by a country, but rather that these countries express a degree of *ownership* when engaged in their relationships. Here, autonomy is very much distinguished from 'autarky', whereby external relations are not *in themselves* sufficient for a country's autonomous status to be compromised. If anything – as the very aspiration to partake in the EU attests – relationships can be an essential means through which autonomy is fostered. In this context, participation in the EU – as a putative *community* that is constitutive of, but not reducible to, its sovereign members – can act as a catalyst for members to express their autonomous capacities through the discovery and sharing of their strengths and vulnerabilities.[7] This necessitates working towards a community that consists of a *shared democratic dialogue* – bringing to the fore the importance of repatriation of the decision-making powers that have been progressively siphoned off to Brussels back to national parliaments.

Looking at the EU as a community necessitates a rethinking of how autonomy is upheld *in practice*. In this regard, democratic inclusiveness ensures that members' decisional and volitional resources are respected and valued rather than being jettisoned *in lieu* of oppressive forms of oversight and interventionism. An awareness of these considerations in the *realpolitik* of political engagement can enhance autonomy, while simultaneously animating interdependence.

In this context, two concepts have remained central to the ongoing construction of its narrative: solidarity and subsidiarity. These values can serve as *relational dispositions* (in keeping with the practice of democratic inclusiveness) through which the EU can provide nations with the opportunity to pursue their autonomous ambitions, secured within the European umbrella.[8] Autonomy's status as relationally rooted can be more fully attended to through solidarity that provides nations with transparent and supportive relationships to engage in. Autonomy's status as an inherent capacity can be more fully attended to through subsidiarity that provides nations with opportunities to exercise their various capacities.

Autonomy and the challenge of Troikanomics
In order to critique the concept of relational autonomy and its relevance to the EU at this point of existential crisis, we draw on the period of austerity. The word 'Troikanomics' is derived from 'Troika', a triumvirate that was charged less than a decade ago with the task of militating against the systemic effects of the European Banking and Debt Crisis; and 'nomics' from the Greek '*nomos*', meaning 'law of'. It is a concept that represents the extent to which, in its structural and operational characteristics, the Troika was a 'law-unto-itself'. It existed outside of established EU mandates and was not accountable to the national governments over which it exercised control, nor to their citizens. It is indicative of a deeper undermining of national autonomy within the EU that is iteratively expressing itself in numerous individual existential crises.

In brief, the Troika was a triumvirate established in 2010, drawn from the capabilities of the European Central Bank (ECB), the European Commission (EC), and the International Monetary Fund (IMF). Its purpose was to provide a 'firewall' against contagion in highly indebted EU peripheral countries by developing, coordinating, and overseeing a programme of conditional funding to be imposed on five peripheral member countries – one that was completely unprecedented in terms of its severity, magnitude, and political oversight.[9] This process exacerbated the single greatest socio-political and economic dislocation in the EU's history by transposing the primary burden of adjustment onto debtor countries, corroding their autonomous capacities.

For millions of people in the EU's peripheral economies, it will stand as an existential reality from which there was little reprieve; for historians it will remain as a defining manifestation of the anti-democratic orthodoxy now typifying the Union's power relations.

In terms of the depth and scope of heteronomy that it has engendered – observable in its antecedents, manifestations, and consequences – Troikanomics provides a timely means of articulating not only the specific ways in which autonomy is vulnerable, but also the *value* that it holds for nations. In this context, impediments to fostering autonomy manifest themselves in more than simply the direct curtailing of *actions*. Rather, nations' freedom of 'will' – for example, in the belief that they had both the potential *for* and right *to* realise their autonomous capacities – is an altogether truer testament of what autonomy demands and what Troikanomics undermined.

Building on this perspective, autonomy reveals itself more so through the deliberative processes underpinning actions than in the act's specific *content*. To put this point in context, in the lead-up to the 'Bailouts' which provided conditional funding under the auspices of the Troika, while countries like Ireland and Greece may have fulfilled criteria for autonomy in a *situation-specific sense* by self-endorsing their actions (e.g., ministers signing their names to the official bailout requests), it is surely the case that they nevertheless may have *still* acted in a heteronomous fashion because the decisional process underpinning their actions had been commandeered by the 'external' forces of the Troika. This pulls back the 'veil' of democracy from what is, in reality, a more brutal process of insidious hegemony. Bailout countries' actions may therefore be seen as heteronomous, because these nations possessed a profound discomfort with their decisions and questioned how authentically representative they were of either the will of their people or indeed of *their own national identity*. Our perspective is vindicated by the criticisms voiced by the IMF itself, both at the time – by, for example, refusing to participate in arrangements imposed on Greece in the absence of debt relief – and subsequent criticisms of the conditions imposed on Ireland.

Troikanomics, therefore, manifested itself as a form of oppressive adjustment under external duress. This perspective is reinforced by purported 'collaboration' on the part of the country – through, for example, enacting legislation to legalise actions that are rubber-stamped by parliaments with no discussion or scope for amendment. This pretence of legitimacy serves only to compound the emasculation of a nation's deeper autonomy.

This has been borne out in numerous ways during the era of the Troika—which was mandated to displace all national decision-making on fiscal policy (undermining countries' self-governance); exclude countries from the deliberative process that should underpin communities (undermining countries' self- determination); and enforce a culture of deference to, and dependency on, the EU (undermining countries' self-affirmation).

This process was disempowering – a period in which nations were constrained from acting on an internal reasoned response to their more authentic dispositions or the demands of their circumstances, but, rather, often in contradiction to their wider set of values, goals, and beliefs. The Troika became the fulcrum upon which their motivations, behaviours and justifications were balanced. It is said that autonomy reflects a fit between who one *is* and what one *does*; in contrast, heteronomy is marked by a dissonance between the two.[10] This oppressive regime resulted in nations walking *away* from a healthy relationship with themselves and a sense of authenticity towards their behaviours, and instead *towards* this state of inner conflict.

While the EU and more narrowly the Eurozone was envisaged as an opportunity for each member to develop their inherent competitive strengths and their capacities to contribute to the wider community, Troikanomics diverted it from this foundational aspiration. The organisational framework of the EU as it currently stands – with an unapologetic emphasis on autocratic oversight – perpetuates an image of the commission as the *sole* agent of community sustenance and cohesion, therefore undermining countries' self-directive capacities. In spite of the fact that member nations ostensibly commune with each other under the umbrella of the EU, it is the EU itself that impedes the reanimation of this purposiveness of community. The irony here is that the EU receives its legitimacy, and attendant authority, precisely from this community.

Troikanomics' influence on the tripartite model of autonomy
We now turn to a discussion on how the experience of Troikanomics scarred each of the three autonomous capacities that nations possess, namely: self-governance, self-determination and self-affirmation. Taken together, these constitute a holistic set of capacities through which a country takes ownership and expresses what it means to be autonomous within the wider hinterland of its peers.

Self-governance is a nation's capacity to critically engage with, and respond to, the range of characteristics that constitute its 'domestic identity'. Its ability to exercise ownership over its distinctive attributes can reveal itself in many ways: in its constitution, its legislation, its budget, i.e. the range of ways that it seeks to engage with its citizens and is responsive to its democratic will. This capacity is a means through which to exercise ownership over, and accountability for, matters within nations' own borders. Governments should thus maintain vigilance in critiquing the causes and consequences of their decisions and examine whether they are in fact a coherent expression of their domestic identity. Self-governance engenders a sense of authority that ensures there is a consistency between the freedoms and responsibilities enshrined in a country's directives, laws and constitution, and their capacity to exercise these in practice.

Austerity, and specifically the injunctions imposed by the Troika, were demonstrably opposed to the self-governance of debtor countries. In the case of Ireland, for example, its banking sector had already behaved in a manner that severely compromised the nation's autonomy – acting against the best interests of the country's status as a small open economy and of its citizens. Troika-controlled countries were deprived of substantive control over their public services, e.g. healthcare, education and social welfare. While national governments recognised the diminution of their executive powers (and the consequential vulnerabilities that this provoked), their hands were tied both by a lack of resources and by the coercive and dependent nature of their relationship with the Troika. Countries under the *fiat* of the Troika lacked the internal instruments through which to counter the crisis in an effective manner, drawing on their own capacities, which they had ceded to a hegemonistic EU.

Troikanomics systematically undermined the principle of subsidiarity, removing countries' capacity to exercise discretion over their own affairs (consistent with the intrinsically cooperative nature of the EU) and discharge their responsibilities towards their citizens. Since neither devaluation nor default were feasible, countries were effectively trapped in a situation that diminished the autonomy and standing of their nation and over which they had no control. This was reflected, as we have noted, in the displacement of the national parliament's role and status as the pre-eminent forum within which budgets were formed and debated – shifting this instead into a complex decision-making process subservient to the agendas and self-interest of creditor/surplus countries. What also merits taking into account, and has been too little acknowledged, is the impact of mass emigration in debtor countries – for which Troikanomics was the catalyst. The exodus of a young and highly educated labour force has contributed to a severe drain on countries' intellectual capital and, by extension, their capacity for self-governance.

Self-determination is a nation's capacity to critically engage with, and respond to, its transnational environment – which, in turn, is influenced by the agendas, priorities, and behaviours of those entities with which it interacts. Self-determination constitutes the primary means through which a country participates in legitimate and authentic dialogue beyond its national borders. It enables these and other interactions to be underpinned by a *critical* stance – mindful of the importance of preserving the country's distinctive identity. It is, for example, exemplified, in diplomatic endeavours and bilateral/multilateral trade relationships with other countries – those occasions where nations reach out towards others. Navigating the demands of their external environment requires nations to *respond* with a sense of political independence and integrity – to assert themselves and have their say, rather than acquiesce in the decisions of others or become sublimated by the sway of consolidation. Importantly, therefore, self-determination is exercised to the extent that countries exhibit freedom not necessarily *from* external constraints, but the freedom to fashion an authentic response *to* such constraints should they arise (uninhibited by latent pressures).

The structure of the Troika – *effectively* operating outside the remits of established EU practices and mandates – was not subject to the same degrees of democratic deliberation that would come with instituting any other transnational organisation. As an 'external' body, its relationship with domestic governments should properly have been grounded in a transparent and collaborative dialogue. The language and mode of enforcement of Troikanomics was, to this extent, disingenuous: it asserted that it was up to the individual members whether or not they wished to remain in the Eurozone, while at the same time, through its governance and its leverage over financial facilities, it made it practically impossible for them to exit without the imposition of the most severe penalties on a country's population. Manifestly, the deliberations and decisions of a country presented with a such a choice cannot be regarded as relational or symmetrical; they are intrinsically coercive.

This response to the crisis was configured around the marginalisation of weaker peripheral countries in decision-making at multiple levels – ensuring that their distance from the centre was maintained at all times (except for the photo-shoots that perpetuate the illusion of solidarity and subsidiarity). Troikanomics demonstrated, in a manner never previously seen, the extent to which power differentials within the EU were rooted in a lack of willingness to adopt a dialogical disposition within the broader ambit of the community. From this perspective, capacities of national parliaments to which we have previously referred highlight the absence of any authentic collaboration – which itself signals the systematic emaciation of self-determination. It is problematic that not alone were such powers siphoned off in the first place, but that this was done in a manner that paid no regard to any substantive deliberative process on the content of budgetary or austerity measures.

Self-affirmation is a nation's capacity to trust in its legitimacy as an autonomous and sovereign entity – encompassing its right to affirm and be answerable for 'who they are' amidst a multitude of other nations. It is expressed in the extent to which nations recognise themselves as being both distinctive in their range of characteristics and capabilities, and yet also as holding an equal normative and political status to other nations – being worthy of a 'seat at the table' when occasions for transnational engagement arise. This capacity presents itself in the collective sense of identification that people experience for their nation, encompassed, for example, in a feeling of national pride or belonging. In practical terms, this is often expressed through symbolic gestures such as national anthems and their flags, as well as the broader showing of support for one's nation in its particular endeavours. In the present context, it was also expressed in marches and protests against the presence of the Troika in people's home countries, highlighting once again the Troika's status as an 'external' and intrusive entity when it came to their engagements with countries. Within the political arena, it is expressed in a calling to affirm and defend the nation and its values against forces that are perceived as undermining them.

Through the expression of this capacity, countries can react to moments of oppression, not with passive resignation, but with a trust in their inner resources as having not only the *ability* to overcome such challenges, but the *right* to do so. Exercising self-affirmation enables countries to retain a sense of legitimacy in spite of potentially difficult circumstances. Without this, citizens and politicians may lack the courage or conviction to rally behind and support their nation in times of threat or coercion.

In both its content and character, the Troika's interactions with Bailout countries, were built on an expectation that nations should express a deference *towards* and dependency *on* them. During the Bailout, it was not simply that countries were effectively denied the opportunity to collaborate on the details of the 'Memorandum of Understanding', but it was the *reasoning behind* this denial that was important. The Troika knew that nations would not (indeed *could* not) be as oppressive and prescriptive in their conditionality for the bailout as they themselves would be, and therefore they sequestered their say in the matter. It was made very clear to the countries concerned that they simply had no other option, that *in and of themselves* they were unable to construct a path away from sovereign default.

The profound sense of loss emerging from this process, whereby the executive abilities of a government were sequestered by an external entity, swept like a wave throughout the bailout countries – an issue which emerges from our case studies of Ireland and Greece. Political autonomy, hard fought and carved out over centuries (such as was the case with Ireland), now appeared to be a malleable concept, subject to whatever was considered the most economically expedient course of action.

The impact of this experience was not given its due regard by the Troika. A country can engage in this form of asymmetric relationship for only so long before it begins to internalise its sense of powerlessness and ceases to question whether an alternative exists to the intrinsically unhealthy relationships that have been established. In other words, a state in which self-affirmation has lost its constitutive meaning and importance.

Conclusion

Autonomy is a foundationally important capacity; it is the means through which nations discover, develop, and share their capacities within and through their relationships. It is, however, also vulnerable. Troikanomics emasculated the substance of member nations' autonomy that had once been taken for granted – it provided a nihilistic demonstration of the consequences of losing the moral compass guiding the EU's socio-political and economic trajectory. It infected what the EU was all about and shifted the locus of responsibility away from the *demos* in individual countries and centralised it within the control of the dominant countries. The EU has embarked on new modes of adjustment and conditional support for member countries.

Nonetheless, Troikanomics remains as a metaphor for the enormous damage to member countries, and to the very EU itself, when the strong discarded the intrinsic importance of relational autonomy for member countries, and thereby contributed to the present crisis reflected in the widespread sense of alienation across the EU.

On a positive note, it is important to be mindful that 'crisis', if reflectively and rationally responded to, can be a cathartic experience that opens up the way to change and, perhaps, redemption. A core challenge is whether, or not, the new Commission and European Parliament are prepared to critique and learn from this catharsis and focus on reanimating the autonomy of member countries by, for example, giving real substance to solidarity and subsidiarity.

Ray Kinsella was an economist in the Central Bank, prior to appointment as economic advisor in the Department of Industry. He was Professor of Banking in Ulster University before returning to the Michael Smurfit Graduate School at UCD. He has published widely on banking, economics and the EU. Maurice Kinsella received his Ph.D. from the UCD School of Philosophy. His publications have centred on the field of applied philosophy, in particular on the concept of autonomy. He currently lectures on applied and professional ethics.

Notes

1   This definition is derived from J Christman's (2015) introductory discussion on the constitutive components of personal autonomy, in which he attempts to bring together, *in an introductory fashion*, general philosophical consensus on the concept. It is the inherent broadness of this definition (as distinct from the definition that he himself develops) that, for him, leaves it open to so much critical analysis and establishes it as such a fertile ground for philosophical debate. (*Stanford Encyclopedia of Philosophy* [Online]. Retrieved from http://plato.stanford.edu/entries/autonomy-moral/).

2   This paper draws on arguments presented in R Kinsella and M Kinsella, *Troikanomics: Autonomy, Austerity and Existential Crisis in the European Union* (London: Palgrave MacMillan, 2018).

3   This model draws on M Kinsella, *Becoming Oneself Amongst Others: A Reconceptualisation of Autonomy* (unpublished Ph.D. thesis, 2015).

4   The influential analysis of G Dworkin, *The Theory and Practice of Autonomy* (Cambridge: Cambridge University Press, 1988), plants the seeds concerning the extent to which we need to understand autonomy – and how it is fostered – as embedded in the interpersonal and temporally extended realities of social ontology.

5   For further insights on this point, see J Christman, *The Politics of Persons: Individual Autonomy and Socio-Historic Selves* (Cambridge: Cambridge University Press,

2009); 'Autonomy, Recognition, and Social Dislocation', *Analyse und Kritik, 31*(2) (2009), 275–290.

6 See J K Galbraith's deconstruction and application on the concept of the 'Conventional Wisdom' (*The Affluent Society*. New York: Houghton Mifflin, 1958).

7 The concept of 'catalysed' is used to distinguish the process through which autonomy is fostered from that by which it is 'created'. In this way, autonomy is an inherent capacity to be exercised through the utilisation of prior capacities, rather than something that is bestowed by one's external environment.

8 For further insights, see A Raspotnik, M Jacobs, & L Ventura, *The Issue of Solidarity in the European Union*. TEPSA BRIEF (August 2012). [Online]. Retrieved from http:// www.tepsa.eu/tepsa-brief-the-issue-of-solidarity-in-the-european-union/

9 These countries were Greece, Ireland, Portugal, Spain and Cyprus.

10 As discussed by A C Westlund, 'Autonomy and the Autobiographical Perspective', in M A Oshana (ed.), *Personal Autonomy and Social Oppression: Philosophical Perspectives* (New York: Taylor and Francis, 2015).

The Contribution of Religious
to Irish Healthcare

Tim O'Sullivan

A recent *Studies* special issue, 'The Nuns' Story: Writing the Record', included a comment by Deirdre Raftery that 'Irish women religious have left a vast, and largely undocumented, legacy to healthcare and education'.[1] This comment could be extended to male religious as well in healthcare, in areas such as intellectual disability and mental health services.

Growing appreciation of the neglect of the contribution of religious has led to significant work on religious congregations in recent years, such as that reported on in *Studies* by Raftery and others. In the field of social policy, there has been considerable analysis of the historical importance of Catholic health care providers in Irish social services, but relatively little coverage 'from within' of Catholic non-profit providers in Ireland – partly perhaps because of their own reticence or their pragmatic focus on progressing the job at hand rather than in theorising about it.[2] Many analyses set out state-centred narratives that view the involvement in social provision of non-profit providers, and particularly those with a religious motivation, as anomalous and distracting from the responsibility of the State to provide basic social services.[3]. Interest in the perspectives of religious has also clearly suffered because of their declining numbers and relative importance in Irish social services and because of grave concerns about the historical abuses in residential child care services run by religious orders.[4]

As a result, although Catholic providers have been a very significant stakeholder in Irish social services, their perspectives on these services have arguably received limited coverage in the social policy literature. Nevertheless, as the *Studies* authors suggested, there is a strong case today for a more balanced reflection on the contribution of the religious. This contribution is not just an historical one, even if the religious orders delivering healthcare are in significant decline in Ireland. An important recent report chaired by Catherine Day on the role of voluntary organisations in publicly funded health and personal social services made it clear that the faith-based contribution to Irish healthcare remains substantial.[5]

This article seeks to reflect on the contribution of the religious in healthcare, while taking account of their own perspectives. It offers some thoughts on the Day report and draws on a 2013 study of my own, which incorporated interviews with representatives of significant Catholic healthcare providers.[6]

Substantial presence of religious in Irish healthcare

The Day report listed seven Catholic hospitals that are still under religious ownership: the Mater Misericordiae University Hospital, St Vincent's University Hospital and Temple Street Children's University Hospital in Dublin; Mercy University Hospital, Cork; Cappagh National Orthopaedic Hospital, Dublin; St Michael's Hospital, Dun Laoghaire and St John's Hospital, Limerick. It also noted that there was a faith-based element in the governance arrangements of several additional hospitals. It referred to the planned withdrawal of the Sisters of Charity from St Vincent's and added that the number of voluntary acute hospitals owned by religious orders may be reduced to four in the coming years: Cappagh, the Mater, the Mercy and St John's (par. 3.3).

In the same paragraph, the report stated that two thirds of all disability services are still provided directly by the voluntary sector, including eighty per cent of residential places. A number of large disability service providers are faith-based, for example: Brothers of Charity Services Ireland, Carriglea Cairde Services, Daughters of Charity Disability Support Services, Saint John of God Community Services. These organisations, the review group stated, account for approximately fifty-eight per cent of the funding allocated to disability service providers under the 'Section 38' funding system.

A somewhat State-centred distinction is drawn at times in the Irish policy literature between large non-profit bodies that provide services 'on behalf of' a statutory body and community and voluntary organizations that provide other services and undertake developmental activities to meet social need without being delivery agencies on behalf of a statutory agency.[7].

In legal terms, this distinction is reflected in the 2004 Health Act. Section 38 of that Act allows the Health Service Executive (HSE) to 'enter ... into an arrangement with a person for the provision of health or personal social services by that person on behalf of the Executive'. Section 39 makes similar provision for the HSE to 'give assistance to any person or body that provides or proposes to provide a service similar or ancillary to a service that the Executive may provide'.

A distinction may thus be drawn between Section 38 providers such as the voluntary hospitals or larger intellectual disability agencies, on the one hand, and smaller local providers, on the other, which are often funded under the Section 39 method, even if, as the Day report noted, some Section 39 bodies, like Marymount Hospice or Milford Care Centre, also have substantial budgets.

What are now called the Section 38 bodies were in a strong position until very recently. For example, when the regional health boards were set up in the early 1970s, the large intellectual disability agencies, not all of them Catholic, persuaded the Department of Health to continue to fund them directly rather than through the health boards. From the providers' point of view, this arrangement provided greater assurances about both autonomy and funding. When that position changed in the 1990s for the intellectual disability agencies, it was only after an agreement called *Enhancing the Partnership,*[8] which provided strong guarantees on the autonomy of providers and their input to policy as well as on agreed arbitration mechanisms in the case of disputes over funding. Before the HSE was set up, voluntary hospitals were also traditionally funded separately by the department rather than by the health boards, though transitional arrangements operated from the early 2000s under the short-lived Eastern Regional Health Authority.[9]

The problems and issues facing religious providers are manifold. In my own 2013 study, one interviewee provided the following overview of what he saw as the difficult context facing Catholic non-profit providers in Ireland, particularly in intellectual disability services:

1. *The increasing age profile of religious and the decrease in religious vocations* (with consequences such as the need to give particular attention to the needs of frail elderly religious)

2. *Social change and the secularisation of Irish society* – leading to major questions about the future role of religious providers

3. *The greater fragmentation of services today and multiplicity of service providers* – in the past, by contrast, there had been a limited number of large-scale providers funded directly by a single funding authority, the Department of Health and Children (although health boards had also funded smaller bodies through what was then called the 'Section 65' and later the 'Section 39' funding system)

4. *Legal issues*, including possible impediments to handing over services

because of possible future liabilities as a result of abuse in the past

Legal changes have constituted one response to the changed context providers face. In recent decades, the religious have sought to protect their assets and their legacy, and to limit their liabilities, through setting up company structures. These company structures are seen as ring-fencing assets, are strongly established in law and have a clearer legal foundation than the boards of management that operated previously. As Robbins and Lapsley noted, non-profit religious providers 'adopted the protections offered by private sector forms of ownership (limited liability status) and ... moved to corporate holding company structures'.[10] Where St Vincent's Hospital, for example, was previously run by a board of management that reported directly to the Sisters of Charity as the owners of the hospital, it was incorporated as a company in 2001 and became subject to company law.[11] The Day Report provides detailed accounts of the company structures currently operated by the large non-profit providers.

Perspectives of religious providers on their contribution

In my 2013 study drawing on interviews with representatives of major Catholic healthcare providers, respondents presented their contribution as 'distinctive', for example, by highlighting their pioneering work, historically speaking, and the relatively late entry of the Irish State in some cases both to service provision and to substantial funding of services.

Examples given by different interviewees of pioneering work by religious providers included the original work of the orders with the poor at the time of their establishment, around the period of Catholic Emancipation, acute hospital investment, the hospice movement, spinal injuries treatment and rehabilitation, the focus of the Brothers of Charity on early childhood development and early intervention and support (in the case of those with an intellectual disability), early intervention with psychosis (the St John of God Delta Services), the work of religious in Ireland today with refugees, drug addicts and prostitutes and the work of religious in different countries with AIDS victims.

Two interviewees argued specifically that the hospice movement would not have developed as it did if it had been dependent on State action and funding. Another highlighted the pioneering role of religious in general and, for example, of the Irish Sisters of Charity in particular, in the hospice movement in both Ireland and Britain and argued that the hospice movement, pioneered by religious, had highlighted the humanity of the patient facing terminal illness.

One interviewee characterised religious as being prepared to 'take risks' in the development of funding – for example in relation to hospice development. Another argued that the investment by religious in acute hospital facilities in the late 1980s and 1990s, albeit on the private side, was a direct result of government cutbacks and mirrored the pioneering investment by religious in healthcare infrastructure in earlier times.

Interviewees highlighted some distinctive features of specifically Catholic religious provision, for example the freedom that characterised the religious vocation – that is, the capacity of those without family responsibilities to be mobile and flexible and their freedom from 'nine to five' routines.

The freedom to speak was also identified as one of the strengths of religious providers: 'Not many groups have the freedom to take on the structures or the officials because they are dependent on them for financial support. You could be in another association but you say something that is not very well-received by the powers that be and your funding can be cut. We are in a position somehow to speak out. That's one of the strengths'.

Several interviewees also suggested, however, that reflection on Catholic distinctiveness should be nuanced and should not be over-emphasised in a simplistic way. Thus, one interviewee referred to the challenging witness offered by committed people of other philosophical standpoints, while another gave examples of voluntary pioneering which were not confined to religious-inspired bodies – for example, the pioneering work of family members affected by particular diseases.

Distinctiveness in a negative sense also attracted comment. Several interviewees referred to the damaged reputation of religious orders as a result of abuse cases and highlighted the abuse issue. One interviewee stressed that this issue should never be downplayed, even if the media, this interviewee argued, while rightly highlighting it, often ignored the good done by religious: 'The other big challenge today, which is very sad, is that … [the members of many religious congregations] did things that really were a betrayal of their vocation and really caused huge suffering. … It is a huge let-down to all of us. But what is not seen or kept in mind is that the number that did do those awful things are a minority but of course they ruined people's lives. We never forget that and that is a cause of great pain. But what is also a cause of great pain is that we are living with that very one-sided view of the contribution that men and women [religious] made in the past and in a different time'.

As one interviewee noted, one consequence of the decline in the number of religious has been the growing involvement of lay people in leadership positions in service provision, including the contribution of lay managerial advisers, two of whom were interviewed in my study.

The legal changes, and specifically the company structures being developed by non-profit providers, were seen as part of a drive towards greater accountability, partly because, as two interviewees argued, these changes had been actively encouraged in the late 1990s by the Department of Health and Children. It was noted that many religious non-profit providers had chosen the incorporated option – that is, of religious providers establishing companies on a 'limited-by-shares' basis.

One interviewee suggested that there was a certain lack of clarity, historically speaking, about the autonomy/accountability context in which Catholic non-profit providers operated. Echoing Peillon's argument[12] about an 'historical compromise' between the State and the non-profit sector in service provision, and other comments on a lack of clarity in the State/non-profit relationship,[13] he referred to an absence, for historical reasons, of an adequate definition of the relationship in the field of intellectual disability: 'Part of the reason why… the relationship between the voluntary and the statutory sector hasn't been defined … is because of the strength of the Catholic voluntary sector in Ireland over such an extended period. It saw itself as being able to define how the relationship would go and therefore it never sat down with the State and the State never sat down with it to work out what that relationship should be in a formal way. The service providers set the pattern because the State had very little knowledge in the field of disability'.

His argument was that there was not a strong tradition in Ireland of looking at *governance,* in the sense of having a detailed discussion of how responsibility should be discharged – often, in practice, strength of personality had taken precedence.

Perspectives on a possible new accommodation
The Day Report, which drew on extensive meetings with stakeholders, offered useful reflections on a possible new accommodation between the State and the voluntary sector. A new beginning, it suggested, should start from 'the mutual recognition of interdependence'. The State needs the voluntary sector

to continue to provide health and social care and therefore 'needs to recognise this contribution and to build a new and sustainable relationship of trust and partnership with the sector' (par. 8.2). Practical recommendations included mapping of service provision by voluntary bodies, official recognition of voluntary bodies through a charter and the establishment of a forum to facilitate dialogue between the State and voluntary bodies.

Similar ideas featured in my own study, where there was also a call for greater clarity about the respective roles of the State and voluntary bodies. Interviewees suggested that such a statement could only come from the state, even if it should be developed in consultation with non-profit providers. One interviewee set out the argument as follows: 'There needs to be a clarification of, and a new accommodation in relation to, where control rests. In particular, in relation to what a contract means for both parties – so when the HSE enters into a contract of service, what is its understanding of its own role and of the voluntary role?'

A new accommodation, he argued, required effort, not just by the State but also by the non-profit provider. He set out as follows the challenge for non-profit providers: 'The challenge for a voluntary organisation is to keep re-emphasising or re-examining its mission, its values, its ethos within the complexity of the environment (such as the political environment) in which it exists. That's what our order has undertaken in the last twenty years – a re-emphasising of our mission. When you know what business you are in and why you are in it, you can make sense of everything else that is going on'.

The importance of partnership was also highlighted by another interviewee, who stressed the importance of a positive relationship with the State as a key part of the way forward for non-profit agencies. She argued that the non-profit agencies needed to cooperate with the State, but also that the State itself needed to cooperate with everyone else. It would not necessarily be a good thing, she maintained, if the State alone acted as service provider – there was benefit to be had from more than one source of provision and a variety of inputs.

Concluding reflections

Reflections on the role of voluntary organisations in Ireland have tended recently to be somewhat State-centred. The focus has been on the State and on its relationship with voluntary providers. The State's prerogatives and the statutory-voluntary relationship are clearly important. Nevertheless, an alternative way of thinking is provided by Catholic social thought and particularly by the subsidiarity principle, which acknowledges the key role of the State but also highlights the critical contribution of bodies coming from civil society.

Vittadini provides a succinct definition and explanation of subsidiarity: 'A democracy ... isn't only the right to vote or to have an opinion but also the concrete possibility to construct social realities according to a shared ideal. This is what Catholic social doctrine defines as the principle of subsidiarity and which implies the recognition of the State not as an end in itself but as an instrument at the service of the person and of his rights which precede the State itself; this also constitutes the foundation of nonprofit activities'.[14]

Such definitions suggest, in contrast to more State-centred perspectives, that non-profit bodies, including religious providers, have the right to take initiatives in response to social need, that society benefits significantly from such initiatives, and that such providers have an important contribution to make to social provision and, by implication, that their perspectives are worthy of analysis.

In my interviews with religious providers, themes such as the importance of focusing on mission, funding problems and the need for partnership with the State were emphasised. A certain fundamental pragmatism characterised the responses of interviewees, many of whom had substantial experience in delivering services and in collaborating with the statutory authorities. This attitude was summarised by one interviewee as involving a commitment to good practice, maintaining the Catholic ethos as far as possible and working side by side with the State.

As suggested in the introduction, there is a need today to document the legacy of the religious in Irish healthcare, but also to acknowledge the continuing, if declining, importance of the faith-based structures that they established.

The 2019 Day Report is significant in that it acknowledges the inter-dependence of State and voluntary sector, including faith-based organisations. It could be seen as re-visiting important recommendations in earlier reports such as *Enhancing the Partnership,* for example, on the importance of partnership, recognition of the role of the sector, review structures and arbitration mechanisms.

Writing in an equally challenging US context, Sulmasy provides a powerful argument for the continuing relevance of Catholic providers in healthcare:

'Catholic institutions help to nourish the faith of those who work in them and are served by them. Our Catholic hospitals also provide a vehicle for proving that our moral convictions are compatible with 21st-century technology, and they embody the ideal that service institutions ought to have service missions. In health care, patients and practitioners alike are becoming alienated from the health care delivery system. Hospitals that treat patients with true respect, recognize their dignity, attend to their spiritual needs, value people over technology and value service over the bottom line are precisely the remedy that people need. Given their mission, Catholic institutions should be leading the way'.[15]

Dr Tim O'Sullivan formerly lectured in healthcare policy at the Institute of Public Administration in Dublin.

Notes

1   D Raftery, 'Writing the History of Women Religious Today: Possibilities and Problems', *Studies,* CVII, 427 (2018), 262–266.

2   T Fahey, 'The Catholic Church and Social Policy', in S Healy and B Reynolds (eds), *Social Policy in Ireland. Principles, Practice and Problems* (Dublin: Oak Tree Press, 1998).

3   M Adshead, and M Millar, *Ireland as Catholic corporatist state: a historical institutional analysis of healthcare in Ireland* (Limerick: Department of Politics and Public Administration, 2003).

4   Cf. Commission to Inquire into Child Abuse (2009), *Report of the Commission to Inquire Into Child Abuse* (Dublin: Stationery Office, 2009) (Ryan Report).

5   *Report of the Independent Review Group established to examine the role of voluntary organisations in publicly funded health and personal social services* (Dublin: Department of Health [health.gov.ie], 2019) (Day Report).

6   T O'Sullivan, *Subsidiarity, Non-Profit Action and the State. An analysis of the subsidiarity provision and of its implications for social provision* (PhD thesis, School of Applied Social Science, UCD, 2013). The interview quotations cited in this article all come from chapter 7. Eight interviews were conducted with representatives of the Sisters of Charity, Sisters of Mercy, Daughters of Charity, Brothers of Charity, Hospitaller Order of St John of God, and the Conference of Religious in Ireland. Five interviewees were religious and three were lay. The focus in interviews was on the acute hospital and intellectual disability sectors.

7   Department of Social, Community and Family Affairs, *White Paper on a framework for supporting voluntary activity and for developing the relationship between the state and the community and voluntary sector* (Dublin: Stationery Office, 2000).

8   Department of Health and Children, *Enhancing the Partnership: Report of the working group on the implementation of the health strategy in relation to persons with a mental handicap* (Dublin: Department of Health and Children, 1997).

9   See O'Sullivan, op. cit.

10 G Robbins and I Lapsley, ,'Irish Voluntary Hospitals: An Examination of a Theory of Voluntary Failure', *Accounting Business and Financial History*, Volume 18, Issue 1 (2008), 61–98, at 76.

11 See O'Sullivan, op. cit.

12 M Peillon, *Welfare in Ireland. Actors, resources, and strategies*, (Westport, Conn.: Praeger, 2001), p.137.

13 See F O'Ferrall, *Citzenship and Public Service: Voluntary and Statutory Relationships in Irish Healthcare* (Dundalk: Dundalgan Press, 2000).

14 G Vittadini (ed.), *Il nonprofit dimezzato* (Milan: Etas Libri, 1997), p.258 (my translation of the passage cited). For a fuller discussion of subsidiarity, see my article, 'Could Subsidiarity Help?', *Studies*, XCVI, 382 (2007), 155–168.

15 D Sulmasy, 'Then There was One: The Unraveling of Catholic Healthcare', *America*, 16 March 2009. Internet version: americamagazine.org

A Persistent Interest in the Other:
Gerry Mc Donnell's Writings on Irish Jews

Shai Afsai

For the past five years, sponsored by an annual grant awarded to my Providence synagogue, Congregation Beth Sholom, I have interviewed and photographed members of Jewish communities in different parts of the world, afterward sharing my experiences in Rhode Island and with readers elsewhere. I have looked at Judaism in Israel,[1] Nigeria,[2] the Republic of Georgia, Ukraine,[3] Cuba, Poland and Ireland.[4]

In preparing for my 2018 summer visit to Ireland, I came across a March 2012 programme produced by Dublin City University's School of Communication and Inter Faith Centre that featured Zalman Lent, rabbi of the Dublin Hebrew Congregation, as its guest.[5] Asked by one of his interviewers about places of Jewish significance in Ireland, Lent highlighted Dublin's synagogues and its Jewish museum, and then added that the city's old Jewish cemetery in Ballybough was a noteworthy place to visit, too. He went on to refer to 'a book of poems ... I think it's called Elegy – Mud Island Elegy – that was written about the graves in the Ballybough Cemetery', which he described as 'quite interesting'.

Curious about this, I searched online for the book and information about its author. Though out of print, I succeeded in procuring a copy of *Mud Island Elegy* (2001), once owned by University ollege Dublin's library, and found it was composed by the contemporary Irish poet and Dublin resident Gerry Mc Donnell. Now a retired civil servant, the sixty-nine year old Mc Donnell, who is a member of the Writers Guild of Ireland and the Irish Writers' Union, subsequently wrote a number of other Jewish-related works put out by the Belfast-based Lapwing Publications.

Mc Donnell's Lapwing oeuvre includes *Lost and Found* (2003), an extended poem about Mono, a homeless Jewish man living in Dublin's Phoenix Park and intimated to perhaps be one of the thirty-six righteous ones that, in rabbinic lore, ensure the continued existence of the world; *James Joyce: Jewish Influences in Ulysses* (2004), a poetry and short essays chapbook revolving around Joyce's choice to give Leopold Bloom, the protagonist of his sprawling stream-of-consciousness novel, an ethnically Jewish background; and *I Heard an Irish Jew* (2015), a collection of poems and prose with Jewish content.

Having in due course become acquainted with several of his works, I hoped I might be able to see Mc Donnell when I arrived in Ireland, but my initial emails to him were all returned undelivered. Eventually, with the help of Lapwing's Dennis Greig – who shares Mc Donnell's curiosity about the Jewish people – I was able to inform Mc Donnell of my desire to connect in Dublin and discuss his work. 'I've received your correspondence from Lapwing Publications. I would like to meet you', Mc Donnell informed me in an email. 'I was thinking of the Westin Hotel on Westmoreland Street near Trinity College. I haven't been in it recently but my memory of it is a spacious and quiet hotel. We should be able to find a suitable spot in which to talk'.

First encounter
On the agreed day, I made my way to the Westin Hotel from Trinity College's Manuscript and Archives Research Library, adjoining the famous Long Room, to which I had been granted access during my stay in Dublin in order to gain information on Theodore Lewis, the Dublin-born and Trinity College-educated rabbi who moved to Rhode Island and then served as spiritual leader of Newport's Touro Synagogue for thirty-six years.[6]

The Westin Hotel is indeed spacious. After I located Mc Donnell – white-bearded, bespectacled, wearing a blue fedora, blue shirt and blue slacks – we found a quiet spot to sit. I had been looking forward to a pint of beer or a shot of whiskey with the author following my research at Trinity College's library, but he informed me that he gave up alcohol years ago. We ordered coffee and cookies.

I had asked him for a copy of one of his works that I was not able to purchase, *Martin Incidentally: A Novella* (2013), which concludes with a short story related to Ireland's failure to aid Jews trying to flee the Nazis during the Second World War. He presented me with the novella and in addition gave me a 2016 Romanian translation of *I Heard an Irish Jew* (in this case titled *I Heard an Irish Hebrew – Auzit un evreu irlandez*).

The Romanian edition's front cover displays a black and white photograph of one of Ireland's most famous Jews, Yitzhak HaLevi Herzog, the Polish-born rabbi who lived in Ireland for twenty years, became Chief Rabbi of Ireland, was later appointed Ashkenazi Chief Rabbi of British Mandate Palestine, and then became the first Ashkenazi Chief Rabbi of the State of Israel. The rabbi's Belfast-born and Dublin-raised son, Chaim Herzog, was Israel's sixth president; the rabbi's grandson, Isaac 'Bougie' Herzog, who was formerly chairman of Israel's Labour party, currently chairs the Jewish Agency for Israel.

In the introduction to *Mud Island Elegy*, Mc Donnell describes how he grew up in the area of Dublin once known as Mud Island, containing the Fairview and Ballybough neighbourhoods, but only became aware of its Jewish cemetery as an adult. 'On Fairview Strand, where at one time the sea lapped the shore, is a curious house with a more curious date over the door. As a child I wondered at this date which reads 5618. I wondered was it 1856 in reverse', Mc Donnell recollects in the introduction. 'The puzzle over that date, cut in stone, remained unsolved for me until recent times. I discovered that the house is the caretaker's house for a Jewish cemetery which lies behind it' (p.9). (His numerical transposition was not far off: 5618 is the Hebrew year corresponding to 1857). Mc Donnell's brief essay on 'Jews and Gentiles',[7] in which he provides an overview of his Jewish-related works, offers no further explanation for why he continued producing more of these after *Mud Island Elegy*. And he begins *I Heard an Irish Jew* by stating forthrightly, 'The Irish Jewish community has been an enduring influence of mine. I am not altogether sure why' (vii).

I asked him to elaborate on his literary fascination with Irish Jews. 'I don't know why I was so interested in Jewry, except for that caretaker's door we were fascinated by as kids', he replied. 'I bought a copy of Louis Hyman's *Jews of Ireland: From Earliest Times to the Year 1910* from the mother of a friend of mine. It had a registry of deaths and my imagination just went wild with it'.

Joyce's decision to place a character with an ethnically Jewish background at the centre of *Ulysses* – in part because he wanted a character who was a foreigner, representing the unknown and arousing the contempt of his Dublin neighbours – influenced Mc Donnell as well: '*Ulysses* and Bloom also played a role. I felt an outsider myself as a writer. I was interested in the Other — in the Jews. In Dublin, they were outsiders. If you wanted a subject to write about, what better one?'

The Jewish artist and scholar Gerald Davis (1938–2005) looked at the poems that would become *Mud Island Elegy* and offered encouragement as Mc Donnell was writing them. 'I used to visit him at his gallery in Dublin, way up at the top of a rickety staircase', Mc Donnell recalled. In the forward to *Mud Island Elegy* (p.5), Davis speculates on why literature related to Irish Jews emerges from outside the Irish Jewish community: 'Perhaps it is the happy fact that Irish Jews have never suffered as their co-religionists in other countries that has been counterproductive to the creation of a dynamic that might have produced a great writer from our community. It took James Joyce, an Irish Catholic, to invent Leopold Bloom. Gerry Mc Donnell has been similarly moved to write about his Jewish neighbours'.

A photograph of Davis dressed as Leopold Bloom for Bloomsday graces the cover of Mc Donnell's *Jewish Influences in Ulysses*. As Mc Donnell remembered: 'After *Mud Island Elegy* was published, Gerald Davis – he was half-serious – said, "That's enough with the Jewish material!" But I went on to produce other books. I couldn't stop'.

Lost and Found

Mc Donnell's *Lost and Found* centres on Mono, who, as a Jew and as a homeless man living outdoors, is both figuratively and literally an outsider. His very name suggests a person who is alone and apart. Mono's thoughts in the extended poem repeatedly return to what is missing from his life and his surroundings. In the poem's first section he muses – often with references to information from Patrick A Reilly's 1993 *Wild Plants of the Phoenix Park* – about the history of the large park where he lives and about the transformations its plant life has undergone (p.14):

Forty species recorded between 1726 and 1976 have apparently been lost from the Phoenix Park.

Mono has memorised 'The Missing' ...

Bulrush and spiked water-milfoil, ragged robin, giant hogweed, eyebright, common whitlow grass, thyme-leaved sandwort, bugle, wood sorrel, yellow pimpernel, rose of Sharon ...

One evening in the park, during the Jewish Festival of Booths/Tabernacles, Mono sees a tent and a man warming himself beside a fire. Mono 'is reminded of the forty years sojourn in the wilderness' during which the Israelites dwelt in booths after leaving Egypt. He is missing a traditional booth dwelling in which to spend the holiday, and has none of the four plant species with which it is celebrated. Mono approaches the man, who invites him to tea. After departing from the hospitable stranger, Mono returns in his solitude to those thoughts of the park's missing species ('the missing'), placing them in a biblical context (p.19):

Alone again Mono thinks about
the forty missing species, the forty years in the wilderness,
the forty days and forty nights,
and the seven hundred and seven hectares
of elevated ground –

the tired streets below.

'The Missing'

This motif of absence returns more poignantly in 'The Missing', the final poem of *I Heard an Irish Jew* (pp.51–52),[8] which references Celtic mythology – suggesting a kinship between the Lost Tribes of Israel and the Irish – as part of a crushing critique of the way Irish bureaucracy prevented Jews from finding refuge outside Nazi-controlled Europe. Here it is French Jews who are missing, because they have been murdered:

The children of the tribe of Dan
of the Tuatha De Danann,
Esther in the middle
the twins David and Michael on either side
and Daniel in front of her
came to our door
and we closed it on them.
The birds stopped singing
and never sang again.

It's five to five on a Friday
close of business;
stamp the permit for God's sake!

The children of the tribe of Dan
of the Tuatha De Dannan
of Le Marais in Paris
went to school that morning
kissed by their mothers.
By lunch time
they were gone
in the thundering trucks.
Each child was chained to the other,
Esther in the middle
the twins David and Michael on either side
and Daniel in front of her.
When the silver chains were broken
they became withered people.
The birds stopped singing
and never sang again.

It's five to five on a Friday
close of business;
stamp the permit for the children's sake!

The children of Abraham
were buried standing;
as were the children of Lir.

When I returned to Rhode Island, Mc Donnell sent me an as yet unproduced play, *Song of Solomon*. As with several of his other works, it has a Jewish theme and – as with *Martin Incidentally: A Novella* and *I Heard an Irish Jew* – is concerned with the consequences of Ireland's failure to aid Jews seeking refuge from anti-semitism. Next, he sent me the most recent version of his *Homeless*. Originally published online as a monologue story,[9] this new version is a one-act play. Though the text still centres on a Catholic character (unnamed in the monologue, but named Michael in the play) who lives in a tent in the Phoenix Park, in the new version biographical details also appear about Mono, the Jewish man living in the Phoenix Park in *Lost and Found*. It emerges, as well, that it was Michael who had invited Mono for tea during the Festival of Booths/Tabernacles.

Homeless

In this new version of *Homeless*, Mc Donnell's motif of missing (e.g., missing species, Jews who are missing because they died in the Holocaust, the living who miss these Jews that are gone, and Jewish political independence that was missing and longed for as an end to national homelessness) occurs again. Michael, who misses companionship, recalls individuals who have broken up the excruciating solitude of his park existence, and thinks of Mono:

> There was this fellah who approached my tent one night. His name was Mono. He said he was an Indian Jew from Bombay. He lived in a Jewish colony in that city. The whole family moved to London. He drove a black cab and took a lot of abuse from racists. He had panic attacks and couldn't drive the cab anymore. He came to Ireland to escape the indignity of being mentally unwell. Of course he was no better here and found himself homeless. He saw my little fire lighting. We had a mug of tea and talked. He was very knowledgeable about the park. It's the largest urban park in Europe. Two hundred year old ash and four hundred year old oak. He talked about the forty species of plants that have gone missing. He knew them all by name – the bulrush, the wood sorrel, the rose of Sharon. He was goin' on a bit! I couldn't shut him up. He said (MIMICKING), *they might again be found in the lakes and the marshes, on the banks of Chapelizod, in the wooded part of the Furry Glen, on roadsides and waste places, in bogs and fens.* 'The missing' he called them. I suppose 'missing' means a lot to his people, the Jews!

The mention here of 'The missing' alludes both to Mono's thoughts about lost species in *Lost and Found*, as well as to Mc Donnell's poem 'The Missing'. Michael goes on to state that Mono 'went off in the dark. I never saw him again'. At the play's conclusion, as Michael imagines abandoning his tent and departing from the park ('Oh, I'll miss my home in the Phoenix Park'), he once more thinks of Mono: 'In spite of many fears I must move on. Maybe Mono will find shelter in the tent. Maybe he will find "the missing"; what we are all finding, losing and finding again!'

That final sentence expressly points to the title of Mc Donnell's extended poem about Mono, *Lost and Found*. Readers of *Lost and Found* know, though, that Mono won't return; he is missing because (like the Jews in 'The Missing') he has been murdered. Sometime after he 'went off in the dark',

Mono was robbed and stabbed in the park by a man who hates foreigners and this is likely why Michael 'never saw him again'. Mono's homelessness and foreignness – and his abuse at the hands of bigots and xenophobes, initially in London and finally in Dublin – culminate (as they did historically for most of European Jewry during the Second World War) in dispossession and murder.

And here I must diverge from the writer and literary critic Fred Johnston's interpretation of Mono's life and death:

> In the People's Garden, Mono is attacked and robbed, not by conscious fascists or insane Jew-haters, but by the Irish dispossessed, the lonely, the outcast, the drink-fuddled, the drug-dead — the utterly uncaring. This is a turn of genius on Mc Donnell's part; nothing separates Mono, the Jew, from the horrors around him, not even his Jewishness. He is gathered up in them — his attackers do not ask about and could not care less about his religious beliefs — and what follows is a consequence of the breakdown of Irish urban society, not of racial prejudice.[10]

The man who robs and kills Mono is indeed a drug addict in need of a fix, but he is also a hater of foreigners. After robbing Mono, he repeatedly demands to know where Mono is from. He *cares* about that. When his fellow drug-addict suggests that Mono is 'a refugee', the man responds with how much he reviles those people. He kills Mono even *after* being given whatever money the homeless man has. His attackers may not know or care about Mono's specific religious beliefs, but insane hatred and racial prejudice are certainly at play in his death.

For what it is worth, when I asked Mc Donnell in Dublin about what leads to Mono's death in *Lost and Found*, he told me: 'The intolerance of immigrants. The guy [i.e., the robber/murderer] just hates blacks, Jews, anyone who is different. Racism, I suppose'.

Taking stock

'Our meeting came at an opportune time in which I am taking stock of what I have written over the last thirty years. There are no coincidences', Mc Donnell wrote me after I was settled back in Rhode Island. A signed copy of *Mud Island Anthology* (2009) – in which deceased Dubliners speak poetry and living Dubliners speak prose – soon arrived in the mail.

I was reminded of how, when we met in Dublin, Mc Donnell had described returning to writing after a creative lull. 'When I went back to write, I went to a writers' group that met every week. I couldn't believe the change in people: they were young, wearing T-shirts, drinking *water*. And they were all writing! It's a different generation. Times have moved on. I'm three quarters of the way into my career as a writer'.

I was also reminded of how, after the conclusion of my hours-long meeting with Mc Donnell and his departure from the hotel café, I had ordered a Guinness and reviewed the notes I had taken. As I sipped the beer I had thought to myself that this meeting alone was worth the trip to Ireland; everything else could be seen as a bonus.

And I am reminded now of the description Mc Donnell gave me of his first visit to Gerald Davis's office:

The gallery was on Capel Street, which was once home to many first generation Jews in Dublin. It was now a narrow, busy, congested street of furniture shops spilling out onto the pavement, a music shop, a famous hardware shop, a pawn shop, three pubs. The Davis Gallery is no longer there. It closed with the death of Gerald. May he rest in peace. I climbed the wooden stairs to his office, on the top floor of the four-storey house over the gallery, in semi-darkness. I opened a door into a room full of half-finished, slashed paintings. Another room had a *menorah* sitting on a polished table and old framed sepia-coloured photographs of what I took to be Gerald's ancestors all around the walls. The stairs narrowed and creaked as I climbed further. I heard a woman's faint voice, singing in what could have been Hebrew. I had no way of knowing. I thought I saw a naked woman leaning against the wall at the end of a corridor. My heart jumped. It was a life-sized mannequin. It was missing an arm and was daubed with blue, black, and green paint. Ghastly in the dim light, it could have been a symbol of all the Jewish women who were murdered in concentration camps. I reached the end of the corridor and knocked on a door. Gerald called me in. I was hoping that Gerald would give his opinion of the poems I was writing about Jews in nineteenth-century Ireland. He was impressed with the poems and agreed to write a foreword for the book and even launch it in his gallery. We had tea and cake which I bought in a Jewish bakery in Portobello where I was living at the time. I walked home along the quays, elated.

I was jubilant as I walked back to the apartment where my brother and I were staying, and eager to tell him of my meeting with Mc Donnell. Perhaps I will meet Mc Donnell again. I always hope for a meaningful connection with some of the people I get to know during my travels. Often this happens, and sometimes I get to see them more than once. After I journeyed to Abuja to learn about Nigerian Judaism, two of the city's synagogue elders reciprocated with a twelve-day visit to Rhode Island, and I saw them again on two subsequent visits to Nigeria; after I travelled to Israel to learn about Ethiopian Judaism, the first Israeli-born traditional religious leader of the community reciprocated with a week-long visit to Rhode Island, and I saw him on two subsequent visits to Israel.

'Abraham Cohen'

I had ordered *Mud Island Anthology* from Lapwing around the same time that I located a used copy of *Mud Island Elegy*, prior to travelling to Ireland. After I had received both titles, I found that although the covers of the two books were different, their innards were entirely the same. The content of the copy of *Mud Island Anthology* I received from Lapwing was actually that of *Mud Island Elegy*. 'You must have got a rogue copy of *Mud Island Anthology*', Mc Donnell said to me when I showed him the two books.

The signed copy of *Mud Island Anthology* he mailed me as a replacement for that rogue copy has thirty-nine poems and ten short pieces of prose. The section of the book entitled 'Lately Discovered Evidence' contains four of his Jewish poems that were first published in 2005,[11] including 'Abraham Cohen', in which a successful doctor muses about two Dublin men less learned or prosperous than he, but bearing the same name:

A Dublin boy, I rose to prominence
as Senior House Surgeon and Physician
at the Metropolitan Hospital in Dalston.
I wrote scientific papers such as
'The Influence of Circumcision in the
Prevention of Certain Diseases' and
'The Vitality of the Jews'.

I am happy to share my name with

> illiterate Abraham 'Miser' Cohen
> who made his fortune from lead pencils,
> and Abraham 'Fresser' Cohen,
> a first-rate amateur cook,
> who failed utterly at business,
> but who could cook fish to a nicety,
> 'very crisp and dry'.

Abraham 'Miser' Cohen narrates his own poem, 'Pencil Cohen', in Mc Donnell's earlier *Mud Island Elegy*. There, Cohen bemoans that even though he succeeded in amassing 'a great fortune' from his pencil business – despite being unable to even spell or sign his own name – he never knew how to enjoy his material success:

> Early disappointments in life
> turned my soul
> … I was grieving early losses;
> black lead on my fingers all day
> and black ink-imprinted sheets at night.

A writer overlooked

That is a dark and apt description not only of a particular Dublin pencil-maker, but also of many writers who work with a compulsion that ultimately lies beyond considerations of financial attainment or literary recognition, and so cannot be satisfied day or night by either. I was glad to find that Mc Donnell, at least, has no regrets about the decades of labour he has so far poured into his craft. 'It certainly was time well spent. It was certainly better than working in the civil service. I never considered that my career. I considered writing my career', he said to me in Dublin, while adding, 'I still feel like I'm outside the inner circle of core Irish writers. I'm not good at publicising my work'.

Perhaps his persistent self-identification as an outsider helps explain why he continues to be so drawn to Jewish characters. Fred Johnston's review of *Mud Island Elegy* laments the lack of attention given to that poetic work by the literary establishment:

> This is a marvellous, brave attempt by, like Joyce, a Dublin Catholic, to recall the identity of the Jews of that European city.

Alas, not enough publicity has attended this book, which is a must for anyone wanting to know more about the nature and tribulation of the Jews in Ireland. Why Mc Donnell has not been interviewed on our prestigious arts programmes or given some space in the 'literary' pages of our newspapers to advertise and explain this little tome is a mystery. Perhaps, to the new, dead-cool Dublinocentric intelligentsia, Dublin's Jewish heritage is not of any value. Not as valuable, say, as the next album from the Corrs.

Mc Donnell's imaginative and informed re-creation of their relationship with the city of Dublin is a small wondrous thing in the welter of commonplace poetry weighing down our bookshelves. Serious congratulations are due to Lapwing Press, a Belfast-based publishing house, who took up Mc Donnell's sequence. A truly *Irish* collection of poems.[12]

Johnston (who is thanked in the acknowledgements page of *Mud Island Elegy*) repeats his lament in a review of *Lost and Found*:

> *Mud Island Elegy* [was] published two years ago by Lapwing. Significantly, Mc Donnell has not been referred to in recent years in any media coverage of celebrations, commemorations or publications on either Mangan or Dublin's Jews. Elites, as well as cultural ghettoes, still thrive in Ireland's capital.[13]

Johnston refers to James Clarence Mangan (1803–1849), an Irish poet with whom Mc Donnell has had an enduring concern, writing a radio play, a stage play and a libretto for a chamber opera (with music by Irish composer John Byrne) that deal with his life and work. Mc Donnell noted to me that the profligacy of Mangan's father, whom Mangan likened to 'a human boa constrictor', landed the family in a hovel in Chancery Lane, a location that also housed Jewish immigrants in the nineteenth century. In *Mud Island Elegy* (p.16), Esther Harris, a Jewish woman who died of insanity according to the registry of deaths, describes her 'plight back then':

> the pogroms,
> the arduous journey from Lithuania,
> housed in a ghetto in Dublin in Chancery Lane
> along with the Italian organ grinders,
> and makers of saints of the Catholic Church.

Not one to give up easily when championing a poet peer, Johnston also attempts to draw attention to *Mud Island Elegy* in a 2008 letter to *The Irish Times*:

Readers may be interested to know of Ballybough-born poet Gerry Mc Donnell's collection, The Mud Island Elegy, with a foreword by the late painter Gerald Davis, which essentially strives to allow some of those interred there [in the old Jewish cemetery] to speak for themselves, as it were. The late actor Brendan Cauldwell read some extracts at the book's launch. The collection came out some time ago, published by Belfast's Lapwing Publications, and was revisited in a series of items for Lyric FM's Quiet Quarter.

Alas, the collection, inexplicably, did not receive any reviews.[14]

A labour of love

Some welcome exposure was given to Mc Donnell's work in August 2017, however, when he was invited to read his poetry at the Irish Jewish Museum during Heritage Week. He told me that he was surprised to find a copy of Mud Island Elegy in the museum when he first visited it. When the museum's administrator told him that she had picked it up at the famous Shakespeare and Co. bookshop in Paris, he wondered how it had got there, but was pleased that it had. When I visited the museum in August 2018, I spotted a copy of his I Heard an Irish Jew in its collection of literature connected to Irish Jewry.

Mc Donnell, who long-ago dissociated monetary cares from his writing, feels fortunate to have connected with his publisher, Dennis Greig. 'There's no way to make a living as a poet. I wasn't even trying to', he said. 'And for Dennis, it's a labour of love. He goes from book to book. I'm in a happy position: I've retired now and can write without worrying about money'. (For his part, Greig told me: 'I was absolutely delighted to publish Gerry's work which focused on Jewish themes; however, there has been no interest in Belfast, even within the Jewish community'. Like Mc Donnell, he views himself as an outlier: 'I am not one of the elite cultural hierarchy here and have for years stood outside the general local literary culture of Northern Ireland').

During our Dublin meeting, Mc Donnell revealed a degree of uneasiness with being a non-Jewish writer of poems, stories and plays about Jews, as well as a recognition that he's selected an obscure subject with a limited audience: 'I've always felt a bit of an interloper when I was writing about Jewish stuff, not being part of the community, and yet I can't really get away from it. With the Jewish material, there are not going to be people queuing up at bookshops, and yet it's what I've chosen to do. Or maybe the subject chose me?'

I am at ease with such resignation and compulsion, and such ambiguity of intent – with Mc Donnell's being 'not altogether sure why' the Irish Jewish community has such a literary hold on him, and not resisting his need to write of it. There is seldom one reason for our actions and passions, yet even one reason sometimes eludes us; our motives are icebergs even to ourselves. Can I properly explain my own interest in the Jews of Ireland and my decision to travel to Dublin, Limerick, Cork and Belfast? Several weeks ago, however, Mc Donnell emailed me a few thoughts about his fascination with Irish Jewry:

> Rumour, innuendo and hearsay were, for me, the by-words when relating to or dealing with the Jewish community in Dublin in the twentieth century. The opportunity to engage with Dublin Jews was further reduced by the fact that the community was diminishing apace. Jews tended to marry within their community as did the Catholic congregation. This kept the communities apart and somewhat ignorant of each other's beliefs and customs. Fortunately this lack of understanding resulted in a deep curiosity in me about the Jews. I didn't feel any of the contempt for them which lay under the surface for a lot of Catholics. James Joyce wrote that this contempt was contempt for the unknown. Thankfully for me this unknowing led to an obsession to know more about the Jews. The Jew Leopold Bloom in James Joyce's *Ulysses* brought out this contempt or hatred in [the character] The Citizen, representing an ignorant Catholic, by reminding him that Christ was a Jew. This was never mentioned in my school days and it became the starting point for my very fruitful journey into Irish Jewry.

For some, the unknown is a cause for discomfort and alarm – for others, Mc Donnell among them, a source of empathy and attraction.

Shai Afsai lives in Providence, Rhode Island. His recent research has focused on the writings of Thomas Paine, Jews and the Masonic fraternity, religious traditions of the Beta Yisrael community from Ethiopia, Judaism in Nigeria, *aliyah* to Israel from Rhode Island, Jewish pilgrimage to Ukraine, and Benjamin Franklin's influence on Jewish thought and practice.

Notes

1   See my 'The Sigd: from Ethiopia to Israel', *Reform Jewish Quarterly* 61 (Fall 2014), 149–168.

2   See my 'Nigeria's Igbo Jews: Jewish identity and practice in Abuja', *Anthropology Today* 32, 2 (2016), 14–17 and back cover.

3   See my 'Uman: Pilgrimage and Prayer', *Reform Jewish Quarterly* 65 (Summer 2017), 162–170.

4   See my '*Jewtown*: Poems of the Rise and Decline of Cork's Jewish Community', *New English Review*, May 2019. I more briefly engaged with Mc Donnell's work in 'Author Gerry Mc Donnell explores Irish Jewry in prose and poetry', *The Jewish Voice*, 26 October 2018, 19; and 'A Literary Outsider, Gerry Mc Donnell Continues to Find Inspiration in Irish Jewry', *New English Review*, November 2018. I thank Lapwing Publications and Gerry Mc Donnell for permission to reproduce selections of his work.

5   'DCU Talking Heads – Rabbi Zalman Lent Interview', https://www.youtube.com/watch?v=zf4gHxEtC-k.

6   See my 'When the Rabbi Told the Truth', *Tablet Magazine*, 29 June, 2018, https://www.tabletmag.com/scroll/265543/when-the-rabbi-told-the-truth.

7   *The Green Door* 11 (2012), 26–28.

8   'The Missing' originally appeared in *The Galway Review*, 20 December 2014.

9   In *The Honest Ulsterman*, June 2018.

10 'Of Arab and Jew', *Books Ireland*, November 2003, 279.

11 In *Cork Literary Review* 11 (2005).

12 'Preserver of the tribe', *Books Ireland*, November 2001, 291.

13 'Of Arab and Jew', 279.

14 'Glimpses of Jewish Dublin', *The Irish Times*, 16 January, 2008.

The Christian Meditation Movement: A Critical Perspective

Alexandra Slaby

Introduction

Lex orandi, lex credendi. The law of prayer determines the law of faith.[1] In other words, how you pray determines how you believe, and how you pray can modify what you believe. Since the end of the Second Vatican Council, which steered the Catholic Church in the direction of ecumenism and interfaith dialogue, and in the postmodern context of an interiorisation of faith, Catholics have been led to 'ask themselves what value non-Christian forms of meditation might have for [them]. Above all, the question concerns Eastern methods'.[2] Fascination for Eastern forms of prayer among Catholic laity and clergy is not new and predates the 1960s. As early as 1943, German Jesuit Hugo Lassalle saw that the meditation taught by Japanese Zen Buddhism helped him deepen his Catholic faith, and his work has been carried on by Belfast-born fellow Jesuit William Johnston.[3] Benedictine monks also have a long history of interest in bridging Eastern and Western contemplative prayer practices – from John Cassian who inspired the Benedictine Rule to Henri Le Saux (aka swami Abhishiktananda)[4] to Jean-Marie Déchanet (aka the father of Christian yoga)[5] to John Main, the founder of the Christian Meditation Movement to Laurence Freeman, his disciple.

It has never been easier to travel East, physically or culturally. At the same time, however, Christians are less well equipped for this spiritual encounter than in the past, when the contents of their Christian faith were transmitted with a reliable continuity in time and space. Meanwhile, Eastern spiritual traditions are valued in a postmodern, New Age synthesis of cultures and spiritualities where ecclesial authority has been challenged and where elements of different faiths and spiritualities can be combined ('Buddhist *and* Catholic') if they offer a new hope of receiving affirmation and healing. Eastern meditation has gained a growing attraction in the Western Catholic world, to the point where it has become a mainstream practice taking place in spiritual and lay settings. In Ireland, it is not uncommon to find

Irish Catholics saying that such a form of meditation helps them in their Catholic practice. The Dominican retreat centre in Tallaght offered a Holy Week session in 2018 called 'Zen and the self-emptying of Christ'. Louis Hughes OP in Kilkenny writes and preaches about body-mind spirituality, yoga and Christian meditation.[6] The Jesuit Centre for Spirituality and Culture in Galway has recently been organising sessions called 'Dive Deeper: Exploring spirituality and ways of prayer' in a 'contemplative approach drawing on Christian spirituality and Eastern practices such as mindfulness'.[7] The newsletters of Christian Meditation Ireland, Irish chapter of the World Community for Christian Meditation (WCCM) show that the group holds sessions in various parishes throughout the country.

These developments unfold at a time when, the Vatican notes, 'it must unfortunately be admitted that there are too many cases where Catholic centres of spirituality are actively involved in diffusing New Age religiosity in the Church'.[8] New Age religiosity is animated by the aspiration to create a global spirituality transcending boundaries between faiths, in search of a common global spiritual core which will unite mankind among itself and with the cosmos. So, when we hear the phrase 'Christian mantra', as proposed by WCCM, not only the Tibetan meditation bell, but alarm bells may ring as well. Can such a word and a practice as 'mantra' be imported into the Christian prayer tradition without modifying the contents of the faith? It is in the light of these questions that I would like to offer an attempt at discernment on Christian Meditation Movement, understood as the prayer practice taught by WCCM.

John Main's Christian Meditation movement
The Christian Meditation Movement, led by Anglo-Irish Benedictine monks, is embraced and established in Irish Catholic life, judging by the frequency of visits to the island by Fr Laurence Freeman and by the invitation of Mary McAleese as speaker at the 1997 John Main Seminar which was held in Dublin. Beyond Ireland, the movement is relatively marginal, but has not been condemned, and its members have not been removed from ministry or silenced by the Vatican – unlike Fr Hugo Lassalle.[9] Indeed, as an indication of their acceptance in the mainstream of Catholic life, their books are on the shelves of the French reference Christian bookstore 'La Procure', and one of them even has a sticker 'Coup de cœur La Procure' ('La Procure's Favourite'). Canadian Theologian Jacques Gauthier, who is very present in contemporary

Catholic life and regularly writes in *Magnificat* about prayer, includes the Christian Meditation of John Main, Basil Pennington and Thomas Keating in his *Guide pratique de la prière chrétienne* which develops all the ways of praying in the Christian tradition.[10]

But John Main's Christian Meditation has also received criticism, notably in France, the home since 2016 of its new headquarters, the Abbaye of Bonnevaux near Poitiers, and also of its most vocal critic, Fr Joseph-Marie Verlinde. Fr Verlinde (1947–) is a priest of the diocese of Montpellier in Southern France who discovered Transcendental Meditation (TM) in 1968 while he was a preparing a doctorate in nuclear chemistry. He then went to live for four years in ashrams in the Himalayas with celebrity guru Maharishi Maresh Yogi who popularized TM. After a spiritual experience during which he rediscovered Jesus, he reconverted to Catholicism. He then attempted to achieve a synthesis between Christianity and TM which was first taught worldwide in the mid-1950s as a non-religious technique for relaxation, stress reduction and self-development. That synthesis resulted in Christian esotericism. But having seen the dangers of such syncretism, Fr Verlinde abandoned that aspiration and has since spent his ministry warning and educating against it.[11]

Like Fr Verlinde, John Main travelled East.[12] After studying for the priesthood and going through a period of doubt about his priestly vocation, he decided to go and study law at Trinity College Dublin. He graduated in 1954 and joined the British Colonial Service. Sent to Kuala Lumpur, he met Swami Satyananda who taught him meditation through the use of a mantra. Main then asked the swami if he could pray with a mantra while remaining a Christian, and he thus brought home a 'Christian mantra' when he returned to Dublin. There, he taught law at Trinity College before deciding in 1959 to join the Benedictine abbey of Ealing, where he was ordained priest in 1963. He wished to introduce the practice of 'Christian meditation' there, but the community refused. Out of obedience, Main then gave up that form of prayer. Then, in 1970, he was appointed headmaster of the school of St Anselm's Abbey in Washington DC. There, after reading *Holy Wisdom or Directions for Contemplative Prayer* by the English Benedictine monk Augustine Baker (1575–1641), he started studying the writings of the fifth century Desert Father John Cassian and found in Cassian's *Conferences* the way to 'recover the unity of his spiritual being' that had hitherto been divided between his allegiance to the Benedictine tradition and his experience of Eastern meditation.[13] Cassian, who inspired the Benedictine rule, recommends repeating a simple formula to come to unceasing prayer. John Main saw there the Christian expression of the meditation practice he had learned in the East.

The *Nostra Ætate* declaration of the Second Vatican Council (1965), which inaugurated Catholic inter-religious dialogue, said that 'the Catholic Church rejects nothing that is true and holy in these religions. She regards with sincere reverence those ways of conduct and of life, those precepts and teachings which, though differing in many aspects from the ones she holds and sets forth, nonetheless often reflect a ray of that Truth which enlightens all men'.[14] 'After that', writes Catherine Maignant, 'everything is a question of degree'.[15] John Main expressed throughout his works a strong sense of the benefits for Christendom and for the world of a common will to recover the contemplative dimension of faith – each remaining in their faith. He returned to Ealing Abbey where, in 1975, he started organising Christian meditation groups. In 1977, he left for Montreal upon the invitation of the local archbishop to establish a new Benedictine Abbey with Laurence Freeman, who was then a twenty-five-year-old monk.

Born in 1951, Freeman followed John Main's classes at Ealing Abbey before going to study English literature at Oxford and then working in banking, journalism and at the United Nations. He joined the Abbey of Ealing as a novice in 1975 under John Main's supervision. Gifted and articulate, he speaks and writes with remarkable clarity. Main took him with him to Montreal in 1977, where he studied theology and was ordained priest in 1980. John Main died in 1982 and Laurence Freeman would pursue his work, giving retreats, animating seminars and teaching meditation in educational, corporate and medical environments throughout the world. The movement, which became known as WCCM in 1991, engaged more actively in interfaith dialogue, notably through Christian-Buddhist meetings. Presenting itself as a 'monastery without walls', it has also developed an online presence through resources such as videos, podcasts, a 'daily wisdom', and meditation support including a virtual timer with a Tibetan bell.

What is the aim of the Christian Meditation Movement? Is it to help Christians of the path of developing their prayer life by showing them the example of the Desert Fathers, whose writings were not hitherto easily available? Is it to promote a contemplative way of life common to all religions? Is it to justify and popularise Main's Christianising of the Eastern mantra? For Main and Freeman, the breach that must be repaired is the departure from the ascetic, 'poor-in-spirit' prayer of the early Christians in the sixth century with the spread of the Benedictine practice of *lectio divina*, mobilizing the intellect and the imagination in the prayerful reading of the Scriptures. In this situation, Main says, 'there is no greater need in the Church and in the world today than for the renewed understanding that the call to prayer, to deep prayer, is universal', a 'deep prayer' which 'leaves self behind' and places 'absolute faith in the power of Christ as the only power that increases the unity among all human beings because it is the power of love, the power of union itself ... The really contemporary challenge is that we should recover a form of deep prayer that will lead us into the experience of union'.[16] To specify the meaning of 'union', 'the modern Christian mission is to re-sensitise our contemporaries to the presence of a spirit within themselves (...)'[17], to 'the awareness of our participation in the life of God, of God as the source of our personhood'.[18] Ultimately, Main writes, we need to 'rediscover the richness of our own tradition, and have the courage to embrace it'.[19]

Hesychasm in Christian tradition

'When you pray, go into your inner room ... '[20] This verse from the Gospel according to Matthew resonates through the retreats preached by Laurence Freeman. He understands it spiritually as the inner room of the heart, the innermost mansion of St Teresa of Avila's 'interior castle'. So once in the 'inner room', how to pray? Precise instructions entitled 'How to meditate' feature in each publication by WCCM:

> Sit down. Sit still and upright. Close your eyes lightly. Sit relaxed but alert. Silently, interiorly begin to say a single word. We recommend the prayer-phrase 'Maranatha.' [I Cor 16:22; Ap 20:22] Recite it as four syllables of equal length. Listen to it as you say it, gently but continuously. Do not think or imagine anything – spiritual or otherwise. If thoughts and images come, these are distractions at the time of meditation, so keep returning to simply saying the word. Meditate each morning and evening for between twenty and thirty minutes.[21]

Is this way of praying rooted in Christian hesychasm or the Hindu mantric recitation, or can it combine elements of both in a way that is compatible with Christian theology? Hesychasm is an attitude resting upon 'objective anachoresis and inner asceticism', 'the two fundamental obligations of monastic life'. It is a way of life that requires 'apatheia, mastering of passions, indifference to cares, discerning and eradication of thoughts, and keeping watch over the intellect and the heart. The goal and the means of these states is withdrawing from the world of the senses and of the imagination to remember God or more precisely Jesus in prayer. Based on a literal understanding of the commandment of unceasing prayer (Lk 18:1; Eph 6:18; 1 Th 5:17), meditative prayer (*meletè*) consists in the oral repetition or mental rumination of a formula, generally taken from the Psalms or from the Gospels.[22] The Eastern Christian 'Jesus prayer' recommended by the Desert Fathers in the fourth century as a method to humbly open the heart to God's grace, 'Jesus Christ son of God, have mercy on me, a sinner' (Lk 18: 10–14), was seen as leading to a state of continuous prayer, of 'prayer of the heart'.

John Cassian recommended the prayer 'God come to my aid, Lord make haste to help us' (Ps 49). Such ways of prayer stem from a theology where God is believed to be present first and foremost in his name, in the invocation of his person, and from a Christian anthropology based on the transfiguration of the body, the awakening of spiritual senses and on the heart as a projection of the *noûs* and of the human totality. Such a theology did not develop in the Western Christian world as it did in the East. In the seventh century, John Climacus saw meditative prayer as a continuous service of God, where 'the remembrance of Jesus [may] become *one with your breathing*'.[23] Based on the *On Holy Prayer and Attention* by Symeon the New Theologian and *Watchfulness and the Guarding of the Heart*[24] by Nikephoros the Hesychast (circa thirteenth century), as well as texts by Gregory of Sinaï (circa thirteenth–fourteenth centuries) entitled *On Prayer* and which are included in the *Philokalia*, the practice of prayer involved withdrawing into a dark cell, sitting down, bowing one's head, controlling one's breath, looking into one's heart and repeating the prayer formula constantly. The aim of unceasing prayer was to open the heart to grace. There was a renaissance of hesychasm in the fourteenth century on Mount Athos, which complemented the Jesus prayer with a psychosomatic technique and gave rise to an 'hesychastic controversy'. When the *Philokalia* was published in 1782, it provided an encyclopaedia of hesychasm and an anthology of Orthodox spiritual texts which showed that hesychasm was not to be reduced to an infra-religious technique.

But only in the twentieth and early twenty-first centuries, thanks to new translations and to interest by Popes John Paul II and Benedict XVI, were the Desert Fathers and the prayer of the heart popularised beyond monastic communities and seminary libraries. In a tribute to John Cassian and John

Main for their contributions to enriching the Benedictine prayer tradition and his own prayer life, Adalbert de Vogüé OSB, a historian of monasticism and specialist of patristics, notes that it is 'a bitter paradox that the most ancient evidence of such a practice should be in the Latin language and that it should have been totally neglected by the Latin world. But that this toothing stone has not been laid in vain by Cassian, the example of Main is here to prove it. Thanks to the author of Conferences, the monologistos prayer, as the Eastern monks came to call it, belongs forever to the treasure of the Western tradition'.[25]

This brief overview of the history of hesychasm reveals that Main and Freeman have sought to root their prayer in that tradition and to show Christians how to purify their prayer from all distractions and representations in order to be and remain in a disposition where we listen to God. They constantly remind the reader that 'in prayer we are not striving to make something happen. It has already happened. We are simply realising what already is'.[26] And as we pay attention to the presence of the 'Life and Light' of Jesus Christ in us, 'we pay attention to our own true nature, and by becoming fully conscious of the union of our nature with Christ, we become fully ourselves. By becoming fully ourselves we enter the fullness of life Jesus has brought us'.[27] Becoming ourselves is becoming love. We become ourselves by drawing from our inner source, the circulation of love that is the Holy Spirit which has been given to us at baptism. We are here at the heart of the Orthodox aspiration to divinisation through prayer: 'We are designed to be divinised'.[28]

Beside John Cassian, another major spiritual influence on Main and Freeman is the fourteenth-century English text *The Cloud of Unknowing*, which, written in the apophatic theological tradition, recommends praying with one short word. Main and Freeman also refer to other contemplative authors for whom prayer is a silent, humble disposition of the soul to the operation of grace. They make frequent references to another English fourteenth-century spiritual author, Walter Hilton, to St John of the Cross, St Teresa of Avila, and in the twentieth century to Thomas Merton and Simone Weil, to show their spiritual journeys of purification in various times and places, and their search for the source of spiritual vitality in their 'inner rooms'. In form and in claim of spiritual ancestry, John Main's Christian Meditation then seems to offer every assurance of adding a chapter to the long history of the Christian spiritual history.

Making distinctions
The discovery by Christians through the prayer of the Desert Fathers that they are placed on a path of 'divinisation' can lead to confusion, if it is not underpinned by clear ideas of the human being and of God which help to discriminate between theologies and anthropologies belonging to the Christian tradition, on the one hand, and imports from Eastern and New Age movements, on the other, the latter relying on different ideas of the human being, God, and the relationship between the two. Two texts published by the Vatican help us make critical distinctions.

In 1989, Cardinal Ratzinger, then Prefect for the Congregation for the Doctrine of the Faith, published a *Letter to the Bishops of the Catholic Church on some Aspects of Christian Meditation.*[29] In 2003, the Pontifical Councils for Culture and for Interreligious Dialogue published *Jesus Christ the Bearer of the Water of Life. A Christian reflection on the New Age.*[30] Neither John Main's Christian Meditation nor Cistercian Thomas Keating's Centering Prayer – the other Christian meditation movement – are explicitly mentioned in the Vatican texts. They are therefore not condemned. But in the grey area where the line between divinisation and cosmic dilution of self becomes blurred, these texts help us discern what is 'faithful to the truth revealed by Jesus' in those meditation methods, and how they can enrich the 'intimate nature of Christian prayer' defined as 'the communion of redeemed creatures with the Persons of the Trinity'.[31]

The Vatican text on New Age spirituality asks critical questions about the ideas of God and of the human being when we enter into prayer: 'Is God a being with whom we have a relationship or something to be used or a force to be harnessed?' Christian Meditation places 'absolute faith in the *power* of Christ as the only power that increases the *unity* among all human beings because it is the *power* of love, the power of *union* itself'.[32] The word 'power' may be confusing, as well as the words 'unity' and 'union'. Indeed, in Main and Freeman's writings, Christ is *both* personal *and* cosmic. Freeman often juxtaposes references to Christ with references to the Hindu spiritual tradition, appearing to posit an equivalence between them: 'As the Upanishads describe, the infinitely small and the infinitely great are the same thing. Or as the New Testament says, the Christ within us *is* the Cosmic Christ'.[33]

These questions are aspects of a theology of 'unity' articulated in the writings of Main and Freeman which can sound problematic when we read that it takes its reference from the Upanishads, with which John Main compares the Pauline theme of the unity of Christians in the body of Christ.[34] Doing that, Freeman only loosely draws on St Paul for whom the cosmic role of Christ has a very specific meaning. St Paul teaches that if 'all of God's creation is groaning in expectation of the redemption of the body' (Rom 8:19–23), this unity cannot be understood as physical; it is 'mystical', although the word came into use later. This mystical union was formed by our baptism 'in one Spirit to form one body' (1 Cor 1:13). The one body of this mystical union is the Church (1 Cor 12:27–28). 'The corporate union of all Christians must grow to fill out the whole Christ, the *pleroma* of the cosmic Christ' (Eph 1:23). For St Paul, the created cosmos is the place where human salvation takes place; it shares in 'the reconciliation of sinful humanity achieved by Christ'.[35] Indeed, 'In Christ God was reconciling the world to himself' (2 Cor 5:19).[36]

When he extends cosmic reconciliation of God with his creation to non-humans, and thus invites us to form a mystical bond with non-human beings supposed also to be made 'in the image of God', Freeman freely adapts Pauline theology. He calls on people of different religions to listen to the '*deep resonances*' that 'can be detected despite the impossibility of ever achieving an exact translation between them ... We discover in the realm of difference itself the mystery of a *common ground*. Within the rich diversity of humanity there is a *unity* that all, even the non-human, share ... The unity is in the inherent image of God that every kind of being contains as its true nature and expresses by virtue of its own unique manifestation of selfhood. This corresponds to the intrinsic emptiness of all beings in Buddhist thought as it does to the atman-Brahman equivalence in Hindu thought. *Not the same, but deeply similar ...* '[37] However, one may ask, how can we find similarities between the God-filled Christian self and the *intrinsic emptiness of all beings* in Buddhist thought?

The anthropology built by Main and Freeman on the cosmic role of Christ can be seen as confusing and as blurring the boundaries between creator and creature in the encounter of prayer: 'We leave self behind; that is transcendence. We transcend our isolated individuality and *we commit ourselves to the whole, the unity in which we are an indivisible part*'.[38] What is this whole? Transcending duality is a recurrent motif in Laurence Freeman's preaching.[39] But as human beings were made 'in the image and likeness of God', when they are called by God on the way of divinisation, they remain creatures distinct from God, and therefore, 'the absorption of the human self into divine self' is 'never possible, not even in the highest states of grace'.[40] The human being is ever and always on the way. Christians are then called to distinguish between *enstasy* (dilution of personal consciousness) and *ecstasy* (preparation for the encounter with the Other); between self-denial as understood by St Matthew (16:24), St Luke (9:25) or throughout St Paul's Epistles, and self-emptying, because 'Christian prayer is not an exercise in self-contemplation, stillness and self-emptying'.[41] But elsewhere in Main's writings, we do read that we are creatures distinct from God: 'The essential context of meditation is to be found in the fundamental relationship in our lives, the *relationship that we have as creatures with God, our Creator'*.[42]

If we look beyond a few quotations – which, taken in isolation, can be misleading – and place the words of Main and Freeman in the broader context of their whole books, and we then try to answer the ten discerning questions of the New Age Vatican text,[43] it appears however that the Christian theological foundations of Christian Meditation are genuine. Adalbert de Vogüé was not worried by that practice in 1985 when he concluded an article 'From Cassian to Main' by saying that there is no doubt that John Main is an orthodox Christian and does not seek to smuggle in a theology that is alien to Christianity: 'Much as we can worry about the way too many Christians resort to Far-Eastern spiritual techniques, the technique advocated by Main gives the impression of an absolute Christian authenticity. It is not his slightest merit – due undoubtedly to his solid monastic education – that he has perfectly assimilated Hindu meditation to a religious life entirely offered up to Christ'.[44]

In a spiritual and cultural matrix where everything can be combined, associated or fused unproblematically, it is the validity of that combination by Christian theological standards that we must question. The place to do so is prayer, where the ideas of the human being and God are played out.

The writings of Main and Freeman provide many assurances that Christian Meditation is about entering into a dialogue with God and not with ourselves. This quotation from John Main cannot say it more clearly: 'All Christian prayer is basically the experience of being filled with the Spirit, and so, in talking or thinking about prayer we should fix the spotlight firmly on the Spirit, not ourselves'.[45] But, a few lines after writing that prayer is 'the experience of being filled with the Spirit', of a 'growing awareness of the Spirit praying within us' (Rom 8:26–27), Main explains that that experience of prayer 'increases our capacity for wonder and our capacity for understanding the *transcendent potential of our own being* ... We feel ourselves caught in the Buddhist *samsara*, the unavoidable cycle of birth and death'.[46] By which Main means, for Christians, participation in the dying and rising of Christ.[47] Following this 'ever-deepening awareness of the harmony, *the creative wholeness that we possess* ... we do not begin to appreciate our own personal harmony alone, but we begin to experience it as a new capacity for true empathy, a capacity to be at peace with others, and indeed at peace with the whole of creation'.[48] Our spirit can *expand infinitely* (*'infinite expansion'*) 'when it responds to the presence of the Spirit of God, from whom it derives its being'.[49] A further illustration of the potential confusion created by language: 'It remains of us only to realize the life He [Jesus] has made available to us, to activate our potential by enlightenment and enlargement of our consciousness'.[50] Also, looking at the table of contents of *Word into Silence*, we see that the chapters lead to 'Realising our Personal Harmony'; but reading it, we see that 'realizing our personal harmony' is about infusing all the areas of our life with the power of the Spirit (as understood in 2 Cor 5:17): 'When a person is united to the Spirit there is a new world. The mantra leads us straight to this centre'.[51]

Sources of possible confusion

The use of the word 'mantra' is confusing. Although here it clearly leads the praying person to the Holy Spirit dwelling in the heart, Main borrows it explicitly from the Hindu tradition: 'The name for this prayer word, called "formula" in Latin, is in the Eastern tradition mantra. *So* from now on I will use the phrase "saying the mantra". Choosing your word or mantra is of some importance. Ideally ... you should choose your mantra in consultation with your teacher ... If you have no teacher to help you, then you should choose a word that has been allowed over the centuries by our Christian tradition ... One of these is the word "maranatha". This is the mantra I recommend to most beginners, the Aramaic word "maranatha" which means "Come Lord. Come Lord Jesus" ... I prefer the Aramaic form because it has *no associations* for most of us and it helps us into a meditation that will be quite free of all images'.[52] The freedom from images, thoughts and concepts is rooted for Main in the 'poverty in spirit' of the Beatitudes, in the 'grand poverty' of Cassian's tenth *Conference* and the asceticism of the Desert Fathers, and in the apophatic theology of the *Cloud of Unknowing*.

However, Main chooses to depart from Cassian by overlooking the fact that, for Cassian, not any prayer formula would do, but this one in particular: *Deus in adjutorium meum intende, Domine ad adjuvandum me festina.*[53] If this verse from Psalm 69 was chosen by Cassian to sustain unceasing prayer, it is because he believed it expresses all the fundamental needs of the praying person. Repeating the formula was to make one poor in spirit, humble and open to the work of the grace of God. As Main puts aside the content of Cassian's specific prayer formula, and indeed all content (*'no associations for most of us'*), he brings his prayer method nearer to the Hindu mantra. Adalbert de Vogüé also believes that Main departs from the consideration of the three virtues cultivated by Cassian's *formula orationis*: humility, acknowledgement of the grace of God and poverty of spirit which leads to the knowledge of God. Main keeps only the third one, the simplification of thought.[54] De Vogüé concludes firmly: 'the Christian legitimation of this Hindu practice is the only thing he asks from Cassian'.[55]

And yet, a slight internal contradiction in Main's mantric exhortation confirms that he is more rooted in Christian contemplation than in Hindu meditation: the suggestion to pray the name of 'Jesus', which necessarily carries the images and sentiments of an encounter and a relationship, as an alternative to 'Maranatha' to be used as a succession of sounds devoid of images. Main says that the name Jesus would be another possible 'mantra', and that Jesus himself used in his prayer, namely, 'Abba'.[56] He exposes here the (his own?) difficulty of positing an equivalence between the Eastern mantra and the Western prayer of the heart. Here is where Christian Meditation differs from the Centering Prayer movement led by Cistercians Basil Pennington and Thomas Keating, which also encourages meditators to go beyond images and thoughts and recommends praying with a mantra, on condition that it is 'Jesus', 'Abba' or 'Love', and expresses consent to the presence and action of God in us.

Looking at this sample of Main's writings, we can see how the use of the words 'wholeness' and 'mantra' can be ambiguous and create a potential grey zone where boundaries are blurred between self, God and the world. Meditators could be inspired by Adalbert de Vogüé's suggestion: changing prayer words each day, choosing one verse from the psalm of the liturgy of the day, although that would be a bold transgression of the strict method of meditation.

There is a strong emphasis throughout the writings of Main and Freeman on the method. Main and Freeman require the protocol of 'how to meditate' to be followed literally and unquestioningly. The Aramaic invocation 'Maranatha' ('Come Lord Jesus') roots this form of meditation in Christianity, but the focus on the utterance and psycho-somatic dimension of the utterance of the prayer word, as opposed to the meditation on the meaning of the word, is intriguing. Equally intriguing is the possible coincidence between the duration of meditation recommended by Main and by Transcendental Meditation. Laurence Freeman has maintained, if not reinforced, the Eastern spiritual inspiration. For example, one day of the 2016 Holy Week retreat preached in Bere Island was held in a nearby Buddhist centre and on the website of WCCM one notices that the only photo illustration on the John Main Seminar web-page shows Laurence Freeman with the Dalai Lama, who is regularly invited as speaker. The emphasis on personal obedience and following can be quite disconcerting and give the impression that Main and Freeman see themselves as enlightened masters or gurus of Eastern spiritualities. However, Main also writes: 'Meditation is not a technique of prayer. It is, though, an incredibly simple means of leading us into an integral awareness of the nature of our own being and of the central, authenticating fact of our being which is the Spirit praying "Abba, Father" in our heart'.[57]

Equally potentially confusing is the emphasis on the results of meditation, which go well beyond the fruit of the Holy Spirit to include stress reduction and lower blood pressure and cholesterol. Also, from the communications on the WCCM website, we can notice an eagerness to secure the endorsement of celebrities and the backing of science for the 'health benefits of meditation' – just like Trancendental Meditation. The language used, especially in Laurence Freeman's public speaking events, could lead to reducing Christian Meditation to a personal growth movement. At the same time, Freeman recurrently specifies that the search for these benefits should not be the primary motivation to pray, and that meditation is about *metanoia*, a 'change of mind' and the development of a spirit of love which will 'divinize' us.[58]

Christians are called then to distinguish between technique and relationship with God, between technique and cooperation with divine grace. Thus, while the Church says that the 'search for new methods of meditation' is 'legitimate', while it can be useful to use techniques to relax and focus, Eastern and New Age breathing and stilling techniques should not be idolised and be used 'only as a psycho-physical preparation for a truly Christian contemplation'. Otherwise, attempts to 'fuse Christian meditation with that which is non-Christian', that is, a meditation where human beings seek by their own effort to attain an absolute 'without images or concepts, which is proper to the Buddhist theory',[59] and ultimately to save themselves, carry the risk of altering the contents of the Christian faith – *lex orandi, lex credendi*. Other ways of prayer however should not be rejected simply because they are not Christian: 'On the contrary', says the Vatican, 'one may take from them what is useful ...'[60] 'There is no problem with learning how to meditate', the Vatican repeats, 'but the object or content of the exercise clearly determines whether it relates to the God revealed by Jesus Christ, to some other revelation, or simply to the hidden depths of the self'.[61] The negation of all activity (movement, breathing, thinking) would mean that we are actively suppressing our consciousness and our personhood to be diluted into an absolute. We would then unwittingly be subscribing to a liturgy and anthropology that are not Christian and collaborate with energies whose identity is not clear to us. Such an activity is not innocent, warns Fr Verlinde, referred to earlier. While in prayer as in the rest of our lives lived spiritually, we put aside the petty concerns and restless activity of our ego and say to God 'Not my will but yours', this 'emptying of all that holds us back' and which 'draws us completely into the Trinitarian life of his eternal love'[62] is God's gift, which he is free to grant us, not the outcome of our own endeavours. Entering into prayer in the latter disposition, with an undue emphasis on technique and results, may cause us to fall into a form of Pelagianism.

To answer another question asked by the Vatican of Christian Meditation, it is not about taking us into our psyche, but about being recharged with God's love for us: 'When it is rooted in us, the mantra leads us to that point of unity where we become simple enough to see, to receive, and to know the infinite gift of God's personal love'.[63] Prayer is described by John Main as the opening of 'our mind and heart to the work of the love of God in the depth of our being',[64] as 'the stream of love between the Spirit of the risen Jesus and His Father, in which we are incorporate'.[65] From reading Main and Freeman's writings and acquaintance with their online material and testimonies, it appears, *pace* Fr Verlinde, that Christian Meditation does not lead to an 'altered state of consciousness'. The body and the thoughts may become more still, but the recitation of the prayer word must continue 'faithfully', and so this method of prayer keeps the praying person mentally active and does not lead to emptiness or the dilution of self into a non-revealed cosmic being. While not condemning the theology of Christian Meditation,

Jacques Gauthier warns on the other hand, on the basis of testimonies from Christian meditators, that the emphasis on reciting the mantra rather than allowing ourselves to dwell in our love for God during prayer can lead, in the long term, to 'emotional and inner emptiness'.[66] Where the emphasis falls is critical if Christians are to practise Christian Meditation while remaining firmly based on the foundations of their faith.

What to take from the encounter?

At the end of this exercise in discernment, it would seem that contrary to New Age, which has been described as 'an Eastern formula in Western terms',[67] we could say that Christian Meditation is a Western formula in Eastern terms. Rooted in the Orthodox prayer of the heart, it borrows the Eastern word 'mantra', an empty signifier, while claiming that its method of prayer remains an invocation, the way to the encounter with God our Creator. Christian Meditation re-sensitizes us to the importance of preparing physically for prayer and teaches us how to deal with the distractions, 'petty concerns and ambitions',[68] created by the ego. We cannot suppress them, but we are to exercise 'watch of the heart' over them. We have seen, through its theology and its approach of prayer, that Christian Meditation is theologically Christian, despite its apparent promotion of syncretism. What is critical, says Fr Verlinde[69], is the intentionality of the person praying.

But in the end, it could be asked: why use a language that can create a potential cloud of confusion above the rediscovery of the Christian contemplative tradition? Christian Churches do not need to go to Kathmandu to find nourishment for their spiritually hungry faithful. They have their own teaching on contemplative prayer, accessible to all who are willing to open the Bible, the writings of the Church Fathers and of the Christian spiritual masters, and who are eager to develop an intelligent faith and a discerning prayer life. Meditation in the Christian tradition is Scripture-based (*lectio divina*); Christians then savour the word of God in their hearts. Physical preparation for prayer is helpful in that it imprints in the body the dissolution of tensions, distractions and concerns produced by the ego. Breathing in and out helps still and focus the mind and reminds us of the life given to us by God, and helps us abandon ourselves to Him. Body postures also make our bodies participate, as they should, in our prayer as in our liturgies, for we are incarnate creatures and our whole beings are instruments of salvation. The Churches have a tradition of integrating mind and body into prayer, from the Church Fathers to the Ignatian 'prayer with the five senses' to the charismatic renewal movements, which encourage worshipping with the whole body. Jacques Gauthier regularly writes about the body in prayer in the Catholic tradition.[70] The Christian Meditation movement has complicated the understanding of Christian meditation and has not, in the end, proposed anything new. One could argue that all about prayer is contained in the writings of the Church Fathers, or in later texts slightly closer to us, such as Walter Hilton's *Ladder of Perfection* or *Epistle on the Mixed Life*. Main and Freeman serve as talented popularisers for those who will not read the foundational texts. However, there is a caveat for those who follow Main and Freeman: the method should not be idolised. Here is the spiritual grey zone that this study has sought to shed light on – a grey zone that is at once intriguing, elusive and potentially disturbing.

Christians meditating far from their spiritual base point to a problem that needs to be addressed at a pastoral level. Such Christians perhaps did not find in their Church the fulfilment of their aspiration to a new 'depth' in their prayer life, and to 'wholeness', that is, to the integration of soul, mind and body in their spiritual development. This is the pastoral challenge for the twenty-first century: offering spiritual discernment and faith-based spiritual formation at parish level, reaffirming the Christian ideas of the human being and God. Then, more Christians will discover and experience what Benedict XVI calls 'breathing in God'.[71]

Alexandra Slaby is maître de conférences/associate professor in the Départment d'études anglophones, Université de Caen Normandie. Her *Histoire de l'Irlande 1912 à nos jours* was published by Tallandier in 2016. She is currently researching the work of Irish Catholic missionaries in her native South Africa.

Notes

1   I wish to acknowledge insights received from Fr Hubert de Balorre, Fr Dominique-Marie Dauzet, Jacques Gauthier, Fáinche Ryan, Pat Coyle, and Joe Greenan.

2   Letter to the Bishops of the Catholic Church on Some Aspects of Meditation, Congregation for the Doctrine of the Faith, http://www.vatican.va/roman_curia/ congregations/cfaith/documents/rc_con_cfaith_doc_19891015_meditazione-cristiana_en.html

3   Catherine Maignant, 'Le catholicisme irlandais contemporain au risque des sagesses orientales', in Christophe Gillissen (ed.), *Ireland: Looking East* (Oxford: Peter Lang, 2010), p.44.

4   Henri Le Saux, *La Rencontre de l'hindouisme et du christianisme* (Paris: Seuil, 1965).
5   Jean-Marie Déchanet OSB, *Yogin du Christ. La voie du silence* (Paris: Desclée de Brouwer,1956); *Yoga chrétien en 10 leçons* (Paris, Desclée de Brouwer, 1974); *Journal d'un yogi* (Paris: Courrier du Livre, 1967–1969).
6   http://www.bodymindmeditation.ie/index.php?option=com_content&view=article&id=47:about-louis-hughes-op-&catid=34:information&Itemid=71
7   'Dive Deeper: Exploring Spirituality & Ways of Prayer', http://www.jesuit.ie/events/dive-deeper/.
8   'Jesus Christ The Bearer of the Water of Life: A Christian Reflection on the "New Age"', Pontifical Council for Clture, Pontifical Council for Interreligious Dialogue, http://www.vatican.va/roman_curia/pontifical_councils/interelg/documents/rc_pc_interelg_doc_20030203_new-age_en.html.
9   Maignant, 'Le catholicisme irlandais contemporain', p.45.
10 Jacques Gauthier, *Guide pratique de la prière chrétienne* (Paris: Presses de la Renaissance, 2010), pp.179–180. See also Gauthier, *Les maîtres spirituels chrétiens* (Paris: Editions du Cerf, 2015).
11 Apart from the reference in n.lix below, see also Joseph-Marie Verlinde, *Le Christianisme au défi des nouvelles religiosités* (Paris: Presses de la Renaissance, 2002); *100 Questions sur les nouvelles religiosités*, (Paris: Editions Saint-Paul, 2002); *L'Expérience interdite*, (Paris: Editions Saint-Paul, 2006).
12 Apart from the extensive references in the footnotes, see also John Main, *Moment of Christ. Prayer as the Way to God's Fullness* (1984) (London: Canterbury Press, 2010) and *Fully Alive* (1988) (London: Canterbury Press, 2013). On WCCM, see the WCCM website https://wccm.org; and WCCM, 'FAQ about Christian Meditation': https://wccm.org/sites/default/files/users/PDF/harris.pdf
13 Adalbert de Vogüé OSB, 'De Cassien á Main', *Collectanea Cisterciensia* 47 (1985), 179–191.
14 *Nostra Aetate* §2.
15 Maignant, 'Le catholicisme irlandais contemporain', p.41.
16 John Main, *Word into Silence. A Manual for Christian Meditation (*1988) (London: Canterbury Press, 2006), ix.
17 Main, *Word into Silence*, p.25.
18 Main, *Word into Silence*, p.43.
19 Main, *Word into Silence*, xii.
20 Matthew 6: 4.
21 As in Main, *Word into Silence*, xvii, for example.
22 Jean-Yves Lacoste, 'Hésychasme', *Dictionnaire critique de théologie* (Paris: Quadrige, 2002).
23 John Climacus, *Ladder of Divine Ascent*, 27.
24 Volume 4 of the *Philokalia*.
25 Adalbert de Vogüé, art. cit., 3 (my translation).
26 Main, *Word into Silence*, x.
27 Main, *Word into Silence*, p.18.
28 Laurence Freeman, *First Sight. The Experience of Faith* (London: Bloomsbury, 2011), p.42.
29 Letter to the Bishops of the Catholic Church on Some Aspects of Meditation.

30 'Jesus Christ as the Bearer of the Water of Life'.
31 Letter to the Bishops of the Catholic Church on Some Aspects of Meditation.
32 Main, *Word into Silence*, ix (emphasis in quotations mine).
33 Freeman, *First Sight*, p.29.
34 Main, *Word into Silence*, p.1.
35 Joseph A Fitzmyer SJ, *Paul and His Theology. A Brief Sketch* (Englewood Cliffs: Prentice Hall, 1989), p.46.
36 Fitzmyer, *Paul and His Theology*, p.63.
37 Freeman, *First Sight*, p.11 (emphasis mine).
38 Freeman, *First Sight*, p.29 (emphasis mine).
39 'Beyond Duality' was, for instance, the title one of his talks during the Monte Oliveto Retreat he preached in 2015.
40 Letter to the Bishops of the Catholic Church on Some Aspects of Meditation,, Part III.
41 'Jesus Christ the Bearer of the Water of Life', Section 3.4.
42 Main, *Word into Silence*, p.1 (emphasis mine).
43 Is God a being with whom we have a relationship or something to be used or a force to be harnessed?; Is there just one Jesus Christ, or are there thousands of Christs?; The human being: is there one universal being or are there many individuals?; Do we save ourselves or is salvation a free gift from God?; Do we invent truth or do we embrace it?; Prayer and meditation: are we talking to ourselves or to God?; Are we tempted to deny sin or do we accept that there is such a thing?; Are we encouraged to reject or accept suffering and death?; Is social commitment something shirked or positively sought after?; Is our future in the stars or do we help to construct it?
44 de Vogüé, 'De Cassien á Main'., 6.
45 *Word into Silence*, p.12.
46 Main, *Word into Silence*, p.12 (emphasis mine).
47 Main, *Word into Silence*, p.26.
48 Main, *Word into Silence*, p.12 (emphasis mine).
49 Main, *Word into Silence*, p.26.
50 Main, *Word into Silence*, p.41.
51 Main, *Word into Silence*, p.65.
52 Main, *Word into Silence* (emphasis mine).
53 de Vogüé, 'De Cassien á Main'., 4.
54 de Vogüé, 'De Cassien á Main'., 5.
55 De Vogüé, 'De Cassien á Main', 6.
56 Main, *Word into Silence*, p.10.
57 Main, *Word into Silence*, p.44.
58 Monte Oliveto retreat, 2015. Videos available online: https://www.youtube.com/watc h?v=jv5ZbhWgiGc&list=PLmN5an552ULRYQMsuSvpG8cTrfa-Pp7Q-
59 Letter to the Bishops of the Catholic Church on Some Aspects of Meditation, Part III.
60 Letter to the Bishops of the Catholic Church on Some Aspects of Meditation.
61 'Jesus Christ Bearer of the Water of Life'.
62 Letter to the Bishops of the Catholic Church on Some Aspects of Meditation.
63 Main, *Word into Silence*, p.44.
64 Main, *Word into Silence*, p.13.
65 Main, *Word into Silence*, p.37.

66 Gauthier, *Guide pratique de la prière chrétienne*, pp.179–180.

67 'Jesus Christ Bearer of the Water of Life', Section 2.2.3

68 Main, *Word into Silence*, p.26.

69 Fr Joseph-Marie Verlinde on KTO, May 31, 2009, programme *La Foi prise au mot* on Les Nouvelles religiosités, http://www.ktotv.com/video/00044598/les-nouvelles-religiosites.

70 Notably in *Guide pratique de la prière chrétienne*.

71 Quoted in Benedict XVI's 'General Audience', February 11, 2009, http://w2.vatican.va/content/benedict-xvi/en/audiences/2009/documents/hf_ben-xvi_aud_20090211.html.

The Irish Constitution in Context

Tim Murphy

The Constitution of Ireland: A Contextual Analysis, Oran Doyle (Oxford: Hart Publishing, 2018), xxvi + 230 pages.

The relationship between the Irish Government and the Oireachtas follows the Westminster model of responsible government, a model that tends to produce parliaments dominated and controlled by the executive branch of government. Because in the Westminster system the executive typically has the capacity to guarantee its bills will become law, democratic accountability of government power really comes about only at elections. *Bunreacht na hÉireann*, however, expresses a strong textual commitment to a tripartite separation of powers – Article 6, for example, refers to '[a]ll powers of government, legislative, executive and judicial' deriving from the people, and many other provisions are devoted to delineating carefully each of these three distinct powers. According to these delineations, and contrary to the Westminster model, the Oireachtas controls the legislative power and the government is meaningfully accountable to the Dáil.

The central argument of Oran Doyle's new book, *The Constitution of Ireland: A Contextual Analysis*, is that the constitutional 'master-text' is deeply misleading because the Irish system has in fact a bipartite separation of powers, with the more-or-less fused executive-legislature on the one hand, and the judiciary and courts system on the other. In Ireland there is a highly-centralised, 'sprawling but more-or-less unified governance apparatus, directed and coordinated (to varying degrees) by the Government' (p.111); there are several political constraints on government but more important are the legal constraints, particularly those arising out of judicial interpretations of fundamental constitutional rights. Behind the misleading constitutional rhetoric, Doyle argues, the relationship between the Government and the Judiciary is 'the fulcrum of the balance of power under the Constitution' (p.155).

This is to paraphrase a complex argument and one that the author presents with great attention to detail in advancing a contextual analysis of the entire

Constitution – an analysis that looks beyond the constitutional text to the range of other laws and practices that form the background to practical, day-to-day constitutional governance. The book is part of a series from Hart Publishing on the constitutional systems of the world, which aims 'to increase understanding of the true context, purposes, interpretation, and incidents of each constitutional system'. In pursuing this goal Doyle's crisp and well-written analysis opens with an account of the historical and intellectual background of the 1937 Constitution (chapters 1–2); there then follow accounts of the constitutional roles of the Government, Oireachtas and the President (3–4) and the ways in which political constraints operate on Government power (5–7); the role of the Judiciary is examined in the context of legal constraints on Government (8–9) and the book concludes with an overarching discussion of constitutional change (10). The book is handsomely presented and adorned with a specially commissioned work by the UK artist, Putachad – the image for Ireland includes Éamon de Valera, Mary Robinson, Countess Markievicz, and William B Yeats – and a brief 'Pictorial Narrative', jointly written by Doyle and the artist, is also included. Overall this book is a great success, and extremely welcome as the first major contextual analysis of *Bunreacht na hÉireann*.

Although the origins of the contextual approach to understanding juridical phenomena lie in late nineteenth-century sociological accounts of law, the approach only began to influence common law education significantly during the second half of the twentieth century. One notable landmark was the 'Law in Context' series of books that was launched in the 1970s. The series, which began with Weidenfeld and Nicolson and is now being published by Cambridge University Press, was originally associated with the novel approach to legal education then emerging at Warwick Law School. The Warwick perspective was based on the notion that all legal educators should engage in the process of 'rethinking' their subjects beyond the narrow doctrinal limitations prevalent at the time. One of the leading law-in-context figures, William Twining, remarked in his recent memoir, *Jurist in Context* (2019), that the approach has been 'largely absorbed into the mainstream of academic law in the UK and most other common law countries';[1] this is true enough but most law schools, both university and professional, still prefer doctrine over context. Although there is a great deal of debate about what should be considered in a 'real' contextual analysis, the approach is associated typically with critical strands of jurisprudence, although Twining himself suggests the underlying ideology informing the anti-doctrinal approach is 'a liberal interpretation of the academic ethic'.[2]

Doyle presents the coming into force of the 1937 Constitution as part of an ongoing constitutional evolution and notes that the text contained much stronger nationalist and religious overtones than the preceding 1922 Free State Constitution. While these overtones were required to garner support for the Constitution in the first instance, over time both religious faith and popular support for nationalism declined considerably and there was a concomitant weakening of these elements in the constitutional order: the amended versions of Articles 2 and 3 that were introduced in 1998 in line with the Belfast Agreement are non-committal on national reunification, and religious natural law ideology has been superseded by liberal-democratic values. Doyle suggests that the 'gradual bleeding out' of these elements is part of the reason for the Constitution's longevity and effectiveness.

In discussing the constitutionalism in the Irish system – that is, the ways in which State power is limited – this book deals first with the political constraints. The author observes that the desire of the Government and its TDs to avoid public controversy and be re-elected establishes certain basic constraints, but he argues that prevailing political institutions and processes do not amount to a competing organ of constitutional power. Doyle acknowledges that constraints imposed by opposition parties in parliament and new accountability institutions (such as the Ombudsman) have moderately strengthened in recent years, and that disagreements and rivalries within the Cabinet, particularly in the case of coalition governments (a frequent occurrence in Ireland due to its system of proportional representation by single transferable vote), can reduce the Government's power, but he emphasises that the Government's control of the primary and secondary legislative processes maintains it as the single most powerful political actor. While there are many ways of focusing public attention on allegations of Government incompetence or corruption – Dáil Questions, the findings of tribunals and commissions of inquiry, the decisions of accountability institutions – matters are not always clear-cut; regarding the publication in January 2016 of the Joint Committee of Inquiry into the Banking Crisis, for example, Doyle remarks that its timing (just before a general election in which the Government's principal competitor was Fianna Fáil, who were severely criticized in the report) illustrates that committees of inquiry 'do not necessarily amount to public contestation and accountability for the Government of the day, but can as easily serve the interests of that Government in undermining its political opponents' (p.131). The author underlines the significance of the constitutional conventions of not extending the term of the Oireachtas beyond five years and of implementing the recommendations of independent boundary commissions for Dáil constituencies. He notes also that the referendum requirement for constitutional amendment has prevented governments from accumulating greater constitutional power. Although the Government has in effect the sole right to initiate formal constitutional change, it must secure the approval of the people voting in a referendum, and therefore it typically finds itself obliged, by means of institutions like constitutional conventions and citizens' assemblies, to 'build a broad civil and political consensus in support of constitutional change' (p.212).

Government is subject also to constraint through judicial controls on executive, legislative and administrative power. Ireland is highly rated internationally for its protection of political and civil individual rights, in part because in the period roughly between 1965 and 2000, an activist Irish judiciary developed a doctrine of unenumerated constitutional rights that allowed for the identification of a plethora of rights not specified in the master-text, but justified, according to the courts, by the general reference to 'personal rights' in Article 40.3.1. In 1996, for example, the *Report of the Constitution Review Group* listed a total of eighteen such rights.[3] But the unenumerated rights doctrine never extended into the realm of socio-economic rights; indeed, as Doyle notes, some Supreme Court judgments in *Sinnott v. Minister for Education* ([2001] 2 IR 545) and *TD v. Minister for Education* ([2001] 4 IR 259) – to the effect, *inter alia*, that even a textually explicit socio-economic right like that to free primary education could never be mandatorily enforced – '[sit] uneasily with the courts' willingness to enforce non-explicit rights in the criminal process' (p.166). In the period since 2000, 'the courts have come close to a doctrine of non-justiciability [concerning socio-economic rights], removing all constraints from the Government' in this respect (p.170). During the same period, the doctrine of unenumerated rights has in effect disappeared, and more generally there has been a gradual weakening of the legal constraints on Government, with greater judicial deference being shown than was previously customary towards executive action and towards legislation. Doyle observes that judicial deference to legislative decision-making is typically repaid by political and public deference to judicial decision-making: 'This ensures that the basis for judicial decisions, which often determine matters of fundamental political importance, are rarely subjected to detailed public scrutiny, a regrettable failure of public reason' (p.179).

That there has been this shift in the balance of power between Government and Judiciary since 2000 is no accident, and Doyle addresses this issue head-on in his contextual analysis, which on this score serves to open up important new avenues for debate and research. The Irish governmental power of judicial appointment has in fact been used to shift judicial culture on three separate occasions: first, the appointment of Cearbhaill Ó Dálaigh as Chief Justice and Brian Walsh to the Supreme Court in the early 1960s, which was designed to orient the Supreme Court towards becoming an activist court in the style of the United States Supreme Court; second, the subsequent non-appointment of Brian Walsh as Chief Justice in the mid-1970s, which confirmed the beginning of the end of the Court's most interventionist period; and third, the appointment of five new Supreme Court judges in 1999–2000 which heralded the beginning of the much more deferential attitude on the part of the Supreme Court. Doyle suggests that there is nothing constitutionally 'improper' or 'inappropriate' in any such nudging of Irish judicial culture, because the Government is a democratically accountable actor that holds the power of judicial appointment for good reason, and because all judges involved, whether activist or non-activist, exercise their functions 'in accordance with their understanding of what the Constitution required' (pp.155–6). This may be true but judges in Ireland are generally 'upper middle-class liberals' (p.188) drawn 'almost exclusively from a small pool of wealthy former legal practitioners', which creates a culture in which 'shared understandings and assumptions about the constitutional order, separate from and occasionally in opposition to the constitutional text and the decided case law, can determine the course of constitutional development' (p.155). Therefore, one may deduce, their judgements as to 'what the Constitution requires' will tend ideologically to be those of upper middle-class liberals, the group to which they belong and which they, in effect, represent.

Doyle remarks elsewhere that the notorious left-right ideological 'flexibility' of Fianna Fáil, coupled with the fact that the centre-right Fine Gael generally coalesced with the centre-left Labour Party, has tended to produce centrist governments, and he suggests this is why 'ideological considerations have seldom been a factor in judicial appointments' (p.50). This analysis seems to confuse party politics and ideology. Although political parties are nowhere mentioned in the Constitution, they play a central role in the operation of the Irish constitutional order; indeed, in this book, immediately following the historical background and in order to explain the interaction between Government and Oireachtas, the first matter to be discussed is 'Party Politics' (pp.47–51). But the role of parties is crucial in regard to the practical operation of the Constitution, not to how the Constitution interacts dialectically with political and ideological considerations. The traditional ideological uniformity of Ireland's dominant parties arose partly because Irish socialism has always struggled historically to assert itself against nationalist concerns; and Ireland's historical record of 'capitalist colonial undevelopment' became the foundation for an ideological landscape in which the centre-right and right have been, and have remained, dominant.[4] The ideology of the Irish political centre-right and right is, like that of the judiciary, the ideology of upper middle-class liberalism.

The nudging of judicial culture through 1999–2000 is the intervention that has determined the profile of the current judicial regime, the regime that brought about the current effective non-justiciability of socio-economic constitutional rights-claims. It is worth recalling that proposals for such rights protection were gaining considerable traction before the turn of the millennium – support was forthcoming from some members of the 1996 Constitution Review Group, for example, and the Irish Commission on Justice and Peace published detailed and thought-provoking proposals in 1998.[5] Irish economic conditions have worsened considerably since that time – Ireland has extreme levels of economic inequality and the percentage of Irish people living in consistent poverty in 2016 was 8.3%, according to the European Anti-Poverty Network, up from 4.2% in 2008, with children representing the most vulnerable age group[6] – yet judicial ideology continues to block constitutional discourse surrounding this socio-economic deprivation. Marxist thought continues to provide the best structural description of the Irish economic system, but it is a society which can only be understood more broadly in Gramscian terms – the ideological hegemony of the Irish ruling classes, including its judiciary, is such that Ireland must be a spiritual home, if not *the* spiritual home, of Margaret Thatcher's 'There is no alternative' ('TINA') slogan.

Writing recently in *The Irish Times*, Michael O'Loughlin observed that the Irish ruling classes – those groups who exert control, broadly speaking, over what ideas circulate as well as over the means of production – have managed to impose a hegemony that has lasted almost a century by '[filling] the upper echelons of . . . essentially non-productive professions: the Civil Service, the legal and medical professions, the diplomatic corps, the Catholic Church, and to some extent, politics'. O'Loughlin went on to remark that the sense of entitlement and complacency among these 'upper echelons' comes from the fact that, unlike the dominant classes in other countries, they have never been seriously challenged: 'No matter how arrogant the French élite may be, they have a collective memory of waking up to find a guillotine, or at the very least, a *gilet jaune*, standing at the end of the bed. This forces them to at least acknowledge the existence of an alternative narrative'.[7] Leaving aside the question of *why* Irish culture is politically passive in this way, it is reasonable to conclude that the attempt to effectively shut down socio-economic constitutional rights discourse by means of the orchestrated shift in judicial culture through 1999–2000 was an attempt to block an avenue of challenge to entrenched economic interests. There may be nothing constitutionally wrong in the nudging of judicial culture, but the nudge at the turn of the millennium was certainly interest-laden to the point of deserving much more intense public scrutiny. At any rate, *la lucha continúa*, given that the Constitutional Convention voted by a large majority in 2014 to recommend the insertion of an enforceable provision into the Constitution relating to economic, social, and cultural rights.

Despite the failure of constitutional jurisprudence to address meaningfully the socio-economic deprivation in Irish society, the country's overall constitutional record is positive according to other indices. Doyle observes that across a range of metrics the 1937 Constitution has proved 'remarkably successful and resilient' (p.2) – the average life-span of a national constitution is a meagre seventeen years, after all, and Ireland's ranking in a 2016 Economist Intelligence Unit survey as the sixth most democratic country in the world indicates the Constitution's success in maintaining a stable governance system that generally respects minority rights and personal freedoms. One of the reasons for the Constitution's resilience is its flexibility – flexibility, that is, in the strict, legal sense of being relatively easy to amend when compared with a 'rigid' constitution such as that of the United States (where amendments must be proposed for ratification either by the Congress with a two-thirds vote in both chambers or by a national convention called for by two-thirds of the State legislatures). Irish constitutional changes regarding 'hot-button moral issues' such as divorce and abortion have come about largely through the amendment process rather than through legislation, something that potentially feeds a narrative that political actors have abdicated their responsibility to respond to social change. While there have been clear instances of legislative abdication of responsibility – regarding, most obviously, abortion law – Doyle thinks that this argument is overstated and supports his view with reference to the range of social changes passed by the Oireachtas, particularly concerning child-related issues like adoption, guardianship and parentage in cases of assisted human reproduction, that in effect paved the way for the 2015 marriage equality amendment.

In keeping with its contextual mission, this book is generally stronger on practical information and examples than a more doctrinal or formalist study of constitutional law – there are detailed yet clear accounts of legislative formality and debate processes, for example, and also of the specific ways in which Government power is most effectively exercised in relation to financial matters. There is also plenty of engagement with several ongoing constitutional issues. Doyle strongly supports proposals to establish a permanent Electoral Commission that could provide more unified regulation of matters relating to elections; he argues that, in the deportation context the proportionality doctrine should structure the type of consideration that the minister must give to, in particular, family rights and children's rights and he remarks with reference to the lack of Seanad reform as to how the continued existence of a weak Seanad serves the interests of the professional politicians in the Dáil – 'the Seanad cannot challenge their powers but does helpfully provide a crèche, convalescent home and retirement community for professional politicians, who have not managed to be elected to the real seat of power' (p.68). There is a very good discussion of the changing role of the president, and also of judicial remuneration, which has caused direct conflict between Government and Judiciary. Although it is difficult to argue that judges should not have suffered the same pay cuts as other public servants during the financial crisis, the author suggests that the judicial pay referendum of 2011 is worrying for two reasons: not only has it left control of judicial pay directly in the hands of the Oireachtas, but it has also 'illustrated the ability of the Government to direct popular opinion and secure constitutional change on an aspect close to the fulcrum of the bipartite separation of powers. This may point to a constitutional fragility of which a future Government could take advantage' (p.155).

There are other matters that might have been discussed in more depth.

For example, on whether constitutional rights apply only vertically, as between individuals and the State, or also horizontally, as between citizens themselves, Doyle remarks that, '[s]omewhat curiously, the horizontal applicability of constitutional rights gained little traction outside the trade union context' (p.185). This refers to trade union cases during the 1960s and 1970s in which horizontality was permitted to guarantee, in effect, the right to dissociation, or the right *not* to join a trade union. Such an entitlement may well be widely-accepted today, with perhaps few claiming that individuals should be *obliged* to join any formal associative group, but was its use in the Irish context just 'curious', or was it an expression of the antipathy toward the trade union movement that capitalist interests, including upper middle-class liberal interests, have nurtured since its foundation?

The book's overall analysis is enhanced by an explicit caveat affecting much of what it says regarding Irish constitutional governance. This refers to the results of the 2016 General Election, which led to the current confidence-and-supply minority government arrangement and served to bring constitutional reality closer to the tripartite separation of powers envisaged in the constitutional master-text: 'Without any new laws, let alone a formal amendment to the Constitution, a novel distribution of party-political support at a general election produced a fundamental change in the way in which the Constitution operates.' (p.62) In contrasting the Constitution as it has operated traditionally with how it works with a much greater degree of opposition and parliamentary power, Doyle remarks that it is 'too early to say definitively whether [the current arrangement] has facilitated healthy consensual politics or political paralysis' (p.62).

As regards the future, although the new provisions introduced by amendment in 1998 in line with the Belfast Agreement are non-committal on national reunification, and although Doyle comments that Irish reunification currently 'remains unlikely', he nonetheless acknowledges that 'the ability of the Irish constitution to manage reunification is now worthy of academic consideration' (p.43). Whatever reunification would entail constitutionally, it is unlikely to be a German-type reunification scenario, with adjustments being made to *Bunreacht na hÉireann* to 'bring in' the Northern territory. It will certainly be interesting to observe what constitutional proposals are advanced in coming years by those in favour of a united Ireland, although one can understand why this volume does not engage more with what remains a hypothetical scenario for now.

The Constitution of Ireland: A Contextual Analysis offers a timely interdisciplinary analysis which will be of interest to lawyers, social scientists and other scholars with an interest in Irish public life, as well as interested general readers. It would be ideal for undergraduate and introductory law school courses on Irish and comparative constitutional law; and ideally it will contribute to establishing a tradition of contextual research on Irish constitutional law. Perhaps the role of the Rule of Law ideology as an element of Irish constitutionalism could have received more attention, and perhaps, for such a densely-packed book, a better and more detailed Index could have been provided ('socio-economic rights' and 'Rule of Law', for example, are not included, while some entries, 'rights litigation' and 'Progressive Democrats coalition with Fianna Fáil' for example, seem not to merit inclusion). But the volume nonetheless provides a wonderfully lucid account of the operation of Irish constitutional phenomena.

Tim Murphy is an Irish writer based in Madrid. He lectured in Jurisprudence and Constitutional Law at University College Cork between 1992 and 2005.

Notes

1 William Twining, *Jurist in Context* (Cambridge: Cambridge University Press, 2019), p.164.

2 Twining, *Jurist in Context*, p.164.

3 Constitution Review Group, *Report of the Constitution Review Group* (Dublin: Stationery Office, 1996), p.246.

4 Fintan Lane, *The Origins of Modern Irish Socialism, 1881–1896* (Cork: Cork University Press, 1997); Raymond Crotty, *Ireland in Crisis: A Study in Capitalist Colonial Undevelopment* (Dingle: Brandon, 1986).

5 Kathleen Lynch and Alpha Connelly, 'Equality Before the Law' in *Report of the Constitutional Group*, Appendix 18; Irish Commission for Justice and Peace (ICJP), *Re-Righting the Constitution: The Case for New Social and Economic Rights – Housing, Health, Nutrition, Adequate Standard of Living* (Dublin: ICJP, 1998).

6 European Anti-Poverty Network Ireland (EAPNI), *2018 Poverty Briefing: And Proposals for a New Anti- Poverty Strategy* (Dublin: EAPNI, 2018).

7 Michael O'Loughlin, 'Why has leftist discourse been marginalised in Ireland?', *The Irish Times*, 26 April 2019.

The State of Global Politics

John Swift

Has the West Lost It – a Provocation, Kishore Mahbubani (London: Penguin, 2018), 112 pages.
Fascism – a Warning, Madeleine Albright (London: William Collins, 2018), 304 pages.

Introduction
These volumes by two foreign affairs professionals who also have experience of academic life offer unusual and differing perspectives on certain aspects of global politics in the most recent years. Albright is more finely focused, more interesting on Europe and less optimistic regarding the future. Her warning is essentially against President Trump; she notes in detail the similarities between his doctrines and style, the doctrines and style of Mussolini and Hitler, and those of other twentieth and twenty-first century autocrats. Mahbubani is shorter (only 100 pages of text), more broad brush, for me more stimulating in that he has more new things to say, but equally more things to question and disagree with. Both authors draw with benefit from their own official-level/political diplomatic experiences.

Albright is Czech by origin. Her birth family were exiled twice, by the Nazis and the Communists. She lost grandparents and relatives to Auschwitz, became a US citizen in 1957 and, after a career as a foreign affairs expert in the Democratic Party, was appointed Permanent Representative to the United Nations by President Clinton, and eventually became the first woman US Secretary of State, 1997–2003. Her book is neither a crude anti-Trump polemic nor a scholarly academic analysis. What it attempts is rather a reflection on the principal elements of Fascism, echoes of similar elements in 'Trumpism' and the dangers inherent, therefore, in Trump's methods and beliefs. She is not at all reassuring about likely transatlantic developments.

Mahbubani is more abstract but well buttressed by wide reading and a rich store of statistical material, including surveys of probable future economic and political trends. He is a Singaporean of Pakistani background, who has been Secretary General of his state's foreign ministry, its representative at the UN and twice President of the Security Council. He sees his study as a wake-up call to the West to accept that its era of global dominance is passing, and that its global objectives need therefore to be redefined, reduced and differentiated in its own interest and in the interest of the 10 billion world population which may be reached by about 2050. His second major thesis is that, largely thanks to the West, the position of the majority of human beings in the Rest (his capitalisation), especially in Asia and Africa, has improved immeasurably in the last generation, in the fields of governance, economic development and stability. His optimistic materialism sees little justification for present-day Western doom and gloom, and no benefit at all in the persistent prevalence of such a mindset.

The two authors cover much of the same ground, and the similarities and differences in their respective approaches provide food for thought. Mahbubani deals with President Trump rather summarily, and while he does not spell out in detail that Trump represents something close to the polar opposite of what he is advocating for future action by the West, especially as regards multilateralism and minimalist military intervention and political interference, this is clearly his view. Both have interesting points to make, for example, on Putin's Russia and on Erdoğan's Turkey. They agree on a lot and where they disagree, there are strong arguments on both sides. One major point of disagreement is in their treatment of the expansion of NATO up to Russia's borders after the collapse of the Soviet Union: Mahbubani sees this as a needless provocation to Russia and as an example of Western hubris; Albright regards it as a legitimate response to the justified demands of the newly independent Eastern European states, and as useful in helping to strengthen democracy and to guarantee better treatment of minorities there. Here and elsewhere, she is perhaps interventionist by instinct, less inclined to question US motives and less sensitive to the concerns of states, allies as well as opponents, which do.

Mahbubani

The West is defined by Mahbubani almost exclusively in terms of the US and Europe; Australia, Canada and New Zealand are not mentioned and Japan is treated ambiguously. His analysis of how the West is now losing it starts and ends with illuminating sets of statistics. Between 1948 and 1973, productivity in the West went up 97% and real wages 91%; but between 1973 and 2015, productivity in the West increased by 73% and real wages by only

11%. In 1965, a CEO earned twenty times that of his workers on average; by 2013, the differential was almost 300 times. A final figure, based on Maggie McGrath, *Forbes* 2016, is that 63% of Americans, about 200 million of them, do not have enough savings to cover a $500 emergency deficit. The trends involved here pre-date Trump by several decades; Mahbubani's main target is the political and social 'elites', including the *New York Times*, who failed to 'explain to the masses' what was happening or to raise their voices against their society no longer being run in 'a decent and civilised' way. This latter echo of Orwellian language is from Martin Wolf.

Mahbubani believes that the most historically consequential event in 2001 was not the terrorist attacks of 9/11 but the entry of China into the World Trade Organisation. This addition of almost a billion low-paid workers into the organised global system had to result, he argues, in massive 'creative destruction' and the loss of many jobs in the West. He quotes a report from the Bank of International Settlements to the effect that the introduction of new workers from China and Eastern Europe led to 'declining real wages and a smaller share of labour in national output'; and that this naturally meant that inequality within Western economies rose. He adds that this explains why Trump and Brexit appeared fifteen years later. Working class populations could feel directly what their elites could not – their lives were being disrupted by fundamental changes taking place in the world order, and their leaders had done nothing to explain to them what was happening, or to mitigate the damage. These points are valid and worth repeating, but of course they were not as obvious between 2001 and, say, 2012 as they later became; the BIS report quoted is dated 2017.

A third set of valuable insights has to do with the world's being now a much better place to live for most people than was envisaged even as late as 1990. Since 1990, world hunger is down 40%, child mortality down 50%, extreme poverty over 70%. About 800 million Chinese people have been rescued from extreme poverty in three decades. Inter-state war deaths and injuries have shown significant decreases. Two centuries ago, perhaps 120 million people could read and write: the figure today is 6.2 bn. And, he argues, the improvements are not just material; access to third-level education, to the internet and smart phones, has led to an explosive growth in the world middle class, and to its expectations and values. All political leaders, not just democratic ones, are now more accountable; Mao was essentially a Chinese-emperor figure but his four successors lived and live within a different social contract. The change is greatest in Asia, especially in the ASEAN countries, but also, he claims, in Burma, Bangladesh and Pakistan; and the advances in Africa, in Nigeria, Kenya, Ethiopia and Rwanda, and in Latin America have been notable.

He has no doubt that China will be *the* world leader, economically and politically, in this century. The final quotation in the book is from Angela Merkel at the G7 meeting of May 2017,to the effect that the US decision to withdraw from the Paris Agreement increases the likelihood of a world led by China.

These are Professor Mahbubani's strong points. As regards his weaknesses, he is notably less perceptive on Europe, particularly on EU internal policies, than he is on the US. His comments on the CAP, for example, seem to have been included simply to make a point about North African farmers. He is also inclined to take all official statistics at face value and as equally valid; massaging official figures is a highly developed skill worldwide, as he should know; they have to be interpreted before they are accepted, especially when they deal with subjective material or likely future developments. More importantly, perhaps, the negative side of his clear-eyed scepticism on how certain aspects of democracy work in practice or what a proclaimed commitment to human rights can cover up is that, in my opinion, he consistently underestimates the human cost of autocratic, non-democratic regimes, internally and externally. As befits a follower of Lee Kuan Yew, efficiency in governance is close to being Mahbubani's highest good; but his tolerance for Vladimir Putin, his uncritical admiration of Xi Jinping and the generally positive report he gives to 'benevolent despots' does not sit well with what he rightly says of the non-sustainability and costliness in human suffering of certain profoundly mistaken Western policies.

This book is sub-titled 'A Provocation', so one should not perhaps take too seriously some internal contradictions or exaggerations for effect. But even if he is no disciple of Beckett in respect of 'perhaps', Mahbubani might have been more restrained with regard to certain developments or trends being 'inevitable', 'irreversible' and 'unstoppable'. And it is more than a little odd that an author who asserts that 'History changed direction in the early 21st century' and that 'History has now turned a corner' finds it possible to criticise Francis Fukuyama's *The End of History* as exemplifying Western hubris and causing 'intellectual brain damage'. Lastly, his charge that media reporting of events, mostly negative, conceals and distorts certain positive global trends is fully justified; but his seeking after good news does tip over to an uncomfortable extent into what seems like a wilful parody of Dr Pangloss. For example, it is not easy to explain, at this late date, how he can offer a vision of the global future up to 2050 or later, as in chapters 1 and 4, without including a substantive discussion of climate change.

Albright

The structure of Albright's volume is complex but its circuitous and episodic approach serves her well, adding depth and resonance to the analysis. The book has good notes and a serviceable index. Her introductory chapter draws on the broad similarities which link Trump with Mussolini and Hitler, especially his strident nationalism and his encouragement of popular anger, envy, resentment and fear. The following five chapters provide a summary history of Europe in terms of the rise and fall of Fascism between the early 1920s and 1945; chapter 7 deals with what Communism and Fascism have in common as well as with their fundamental dissimilarities. After a reflective section on the inherent difficulties of democracy, the second half of the book covers modern, fascist-type autocrats, viz. Milošević in Yugoslavia, Chavez in Venezuela, Erdoğan in Turkey, Putin in Moscow, Orbán and Kaczyński in Hungary and Poland respectively and the various Kims in North Korea. She finishes with three chapters on the US, past and future.

It is clear from the first chapter that Albright does not employ the term 'Fascist' as a lazy and generalised form of abuse, in the way that some left-wing politicians and journalists do. She takes care, not exactly to define Fascism or to distinguish it from related concepts such as totalitarianism, autocracy etc., but to list its chief elements as manifested over time. Her lists have the obvious ingredients – extreme nationalism, authoritarianism, disregard for the rights of those outside the chosen group, willingness to use force and covert violence to achieve chosen ends, belief in strong, often charismatic, leadership and strict discipline amongst those led, maximum control of the media and incessant propaganda, appeals to the past and its values, combined with a willingness to overturn inherited norms and institutions when these prove obstructive. Some of her elements are perhaps not so obvious – e.g. that Fascism historically appealed to both ends of society, to those who had nothing to lose as well as to those who had everything to lose; that it appeals to those under economic stress, not just for what they do not have but for what they believe they should have, and have been unjustly denied; and that organised public spectacles, shows, parades and mass meetings were traditionally part of the chosen means to solidify Fascist group thinking and mass solidarity.

Albright is also careful not to simplify Fascism into a creed easily dismissed, appealing only to misfits and the malignly-intentioned. She points out that in Germany, the original Nazis were not only anti-semitic xenophobes; they also advocated higher old-age pensions, better educational opportunities for the poor, an end to child labour and improved maternal health care. It is evident that Fascism brought to many new hope, a renewed sense of community with kindred souls and a fervent expectation that national, social and political regeneration was possible. She believes that Fascism caught on because many saw it as a mighty wave that was transforming history, that was owned by them and by people who thought like them, and that could not be stopped; the impact of 'the future belongs to me' syndrome is immeasurable. She gives credit as relevant in the latter section of her study to the reformist elements in the programmes of the modern dictators, without allowing this to over-balance her judgement.

Her book is embellished and enlivened by a good selection of apt quotations from opponents of Fascism and defenders of democracy. The dedication is 'To the victims of Fascism, then and now, and to all who fight Fascism in others and in themselves'; this is followed by Primo Levi's saying that every age has its own Fascism. My favourite quote comes in the reflective chapter after she has acknowledged that democracy is prone to every error, from incompetence and corruption to gridlock and misguided fashions. It is from Tomáš Masaryk, the first president of independent Czechoslovakia, who said: 'Democracy is not just a form of state, it is not just something that is embodied in a constitution; democracy is a view of life, it requires a belief in human beings, in humanity . . . Democracy is a discussion, and a real discussion is possible only if people trust each other and if they try fairly to find the truth'.

Albright deals briefly but cogently with the European project, migration and Brexit. On the EU, she remarks that it was fear that Fascism might return to the continent where it was born that spurred the drive for European integration. The choice for integration has always had to do battle with existing member state nationalisms, it has always been more compelling logically than emotionally and its Achilles' heel is that it has remained a top-down enterprise. She mentions the illogicality of resentment against the 'Brussels bureaucrats', but emphasises its dangerously widespread and pervasive nature. On migrants and refugees, she admits to strong feelings due in part to her family history, castigates politicians who try to win votes by kindling hatred, accepts that practical limits on 'absorption capacity' can exist, and believes that the necessary goodwill and time are often unavailable. On Brexit she is scathing: noting that wariness towards migrants almost certainly spelled the difference between success and failure for the 2016 referendum in the UK, she describes the results of the referendum as 'an exercise in economic masochism that Britons will long regret'. The conclusion is: 'Grumbling about their marriage to the EU and threatening to leave gave the British leverage at the bargaining table; calling their own bluff and filing for divorce has left them with none'.

There is little enough new or startling in Albright's critique of Trump's views, style and presidency. What she has to say is the stuff of our daily headlines. She begins with foreign policy issues (climate change, Iran, NAFTA, Mexico, Islamophobia) and gives significant space to his admiration for 'strong', i.e. anti-democratic, leaders – Duterte, El-Sisi, Erdoğan, etc. – and his picking of quarrels with traditional friends and allies. On internal US matters, she sees Trump as the first president to consistently denigrate the US courts and due process, the security services, the media and the electoral system. Regarding the economy, his stress on the theft of jobs and the US being ripped off is one-sided, to put it at its mildest; much of what he says is simply false, his language is that of a demagogue, his chief concern seems to be to stir up resentments and exploit insecurities. All of this is dealt with coolly and academically, she gives Trump credit for his few successes and she notes his conviction and consistency.

Albright describes herself as an optimist with worries. She feels strongly that there will be a cost to the Trump presidency/presidencies and she asks herself what will the damage be. She quotes Primo Levi again that a critical point may be reached, not through terror or intimidation but 'by denying and distorting information, by undermining systems of justice . . . and by spreading in myriad subtle ways nostalgia for a world where order reigned'. We hardly need to be convinced. In my view, the best brief judgement on the links between Trump's and a Fascist world-view is to apply to him what Albright says regarding 'the self-centred moral numbness' which allowed Fascism to thrive.

Although the analysis is balanced and reasonably comprehensive, I noted the absence of two important points. She does not cover the failure of the post-2001 administrations, and in particular those of Presidents Clinton and Obama, to explain or to try to mitigate in any substantive way the negative impact of certain world trends on significant sections of the US workforce. On this, I believe Mahbubani's views are correct and that this failure contributed in large measure to the rise of Trump to prominence and to the pressures leading towards Brexit. Of course, by the turn of the millennium, globalisation was a fact and no longer an ideological choice; and Albright does defend President Obama's tax and spending policies as aimed at lifting wages for low- and middle-income people. But if this was the sum of the US effort to fight against the twenty-first century phenomenon of a growing divide between rich and poor, of the rich getting richer and the poor poorer, it was not particularly successful. The US is now, unhappily, a world leader in this division, followed closely in Europe by the UK and Ireland.

While there are some sharply pertinent observations in the chapters on the modern dictatorships (see, e.g., Albright's quite shocking description of the referendum organised by Orbán in Hungary in 2017), one notable absence from these chapters is China, and the Chinese President, Xi Jinping . It is true that Xi is described as the most powerful leader of his country since the apogee of the Qing Dynasty, that a passing reference is made to the standard official Chinese view that human rights in China are nobody else's business, and that the thesis that Chinese-style authoritarianism is somehow a more practical option is questioned. But this is hardly enough. The fact that China is now a world power, economically and politically, is all the more reason why its Fascist-like aspects, totalitarianism, refusal of the possibility of dissent, persecution of minorities, etc., should be confronted directly.

Final Thought

In an impressive article in *The Guardian* on 5 September 2018, Stanislaw Aronson, a Polish Jew, and survivor of the partisan struggle against the Nazis and the Warsaw Uprising, who is now aged ninety-three and living in Israel, wrote of his fears that extremism was rising again in Europe and elsewhere. He asks himself what are the lessons which should be drawn from the terrible history he lived through, which are now in danger of being falsified or forgotten. Among other such lessons, he mentions his belief that truth matters and that lies can kill. His most salutary point, directly relevant to both

Mahbubani's utopian optimism and to Albright's geo-political apprehensions is this: 'Finally, do not ever imagine that your world cannot collapse, as ours did. This may seem the most obvious lesson to be passed on, but only because it is the most important. One moment I was enjoying an idyllic adolescence in my home city of Lodz, and the next we were on the run. I would only return to my empty home five years later, no longer a carefree boy but a Holocaust survivor and Home Army veteran, living in fear of Stalin's secret police'.

John Swift has served as Irish ambassador in many countries and is a frequent contributor to *Studies*.

Book Reviews

Protestant and *Irish: The Minority's Search for Place in Independent Ireland,* Ian d'Alton and Ida Milne (eds) (Cork: Cork University Press, 2018), 396 pages.

In 2010, Ida Milne presented a paper to the sixtieth convention of the Irish History Students' Association entitled 'The quiet corner back: how rural Protestants contributed to the GAA within the 26 counties'. It examined 'the ways in which rural Protestants involved themselves with the GAA – an involvement that tended to be unostentatious but pervasive'. Milne is one of the editors of the compendium of essays under review, which contains further research on 'the concept that involvement with the organisation was a way in which some Protestants chose to clearly delineate their Irishness and also to be part of their local community', as well as the different conceptions of the organisation amongst Protestants on either side of the border, and it is as good an example as any of the many and varied (and frequently unconsidered) experiences of this minority in its search for place in independent Ireland.

Milne's contribution lies in the middle of the three sections into which this book is divided: 'Engagement', while that of her partner in enterprise and co-editor, Ian d'Alton (a fellow of some jest, as his entry in the list of contributors will attest) is in the previous division. Entitled 'Belonging', and deals with the 'coming to terms' of 'this apparently beached people' between the creation of the Irish Free State in 1922 and its departure from the Commonwealth in 1948. Admitting that 'some sort of umbilical cord had been snapped', d'Alton proposes that the emergence of the Republic 'opened the potential [for] a truly common patriotism to emerge' that would lead to Bishop Butler's 'confident minority' just seventeen years later.

D'Alton and Milne are joined by fourteen other essayists between the covers of 'Protestant *and* Irish', the italicised middle word of which title serves to emphasise both the aspirations and experiences of this sometimes embattled group of fellow citizens in an independent Ireland. In a sentiment that will resonate with other historians (and many a novelist), the editors admit setting out to write one book only to produce another, as the contributions received introduced them to some of their own blind spots. The editors' original intent had been to tell of the experiences of

Protestants fitting in, 'not out of a sense of unease, but because ... it suited'. The material received allowed them to realise the same idea in a different way, as they broadened the definition of 'fitting in' to embrace those who found their places both noisily and by 'keeping [the] head down'.

The collection is sub-divided into three sections, the aforementioned 'Belonging' and 'Engagement' and the final 'Otherness', and comprises contributions that range from 'Defining Loyalty' to 'Women and Inter-church Marriage', by way of 'Class Politics' and 'The Life and Death of Protestant Businesses'. 'Belonging' addresses different types of loyalty and 'belongingness' between 1922 and 1948, while 'Engagement' deals with several aspects of Protestant involvement in Irish life from TCD to the GAA. The concluding 'Otherness' addresses the plight of 'outsider' and even 'Double outsider' communities – 'cut off from one community while never quite able fully to enter the experience of the other' – as in the case of 'Protestant Republicans in the Revolution and After' by Martin Maguire.

The sixteen compositions span the decades from the foundation of the Free State to the 1960s and examine the experiences of the Protestant survivors in this period, as opposed to bewailing the losses of prestige and power, not to mention the genteel lifestyle, of the privileged few in the world of the 'Big Houses'. These are the tales of Irish people, who wanted to be Irish, more so than latter day unionists craving for a return to their erstwhile position as residents of 'John Bull's Other Island' (which Shaw had dubbed 'the real old Ireland').

The period in question (1922–mid-1960s) was a formative one for a formerly dominant minority in a new political environment. The volume aspires to tell a nuanced and complex tale and 'present a colourful and intricate picture ... of a community ... delimited both by what it felt it was and ... was not', and in this it is remarkably successful. The editors attempt to correct the underestimation (and under-reporting) of 'the ability of Protestants in the new Ireland to shape shift and ... adapt to local conditions' in an increasingly benign socio-political climate. In 1922 this was a far from homogeneous group as it spanned the socio-economic spectrum from domestic servant, shop assistants and trade unionists, by way of teachers, nurses and farmers, to revolutionaries and university lecturers. Although 'Protestants were undoubtedly more prosperous than the general population', they also included 'small farmers struggling to subsist, single ladies beggared enough to need support from aid societies, domestic servants and an urban working class' – not least Seán O'Casey's redoubtable tenement dwelling unionist, Bessie Burgess.

The volume is not without its lighter side in the contributions of Caleb Richardson on 'the nature of humour and the Southern Irish Protestant' in the work of Patrick Campbell ('Quidnunc' of *The Irish Times*) and Felix Larkin's fine (illustrated) piece on the depiction of Southern Irish Protestants in Irish Cartoons (especially C E Kelly's classic 'Ceilidhe in the Kildare Street Club' from *Dublin Opinion*). In truth, Campbell's cool, detached style very much mirrors that of the editors in their relaxed approach to the essays in their care, as they chart the complex journey of southern Protestants to their 'place in the new dispensation [in which they] are now more or less "uncomplicatedly Irish."'

As Roy Foster notes in his preface, the various contributions in *Protestant* and *Irish* reflect 'a certain vibrancy and combativeness … within the ostensibly dusty and downbeat image of Southern Irish Protestantism'. As the editors conclude, the sixteen essays speak for themselves; they also speak for their authors and for the editors, as well as for the minority under review – and they do so with much eloquence.

Declan O'Keeffe is Assistant Archivist and College Historian, Clongowes Wood College.

Nano Nagle. The Life and the Legacy, Deirdre Raftery, Catriona Delaney, Catherine Nowlan-Roebuck (Newbridge: Irish Academic Press, 2019), xix+294 pages.

In the course of the Second Vatican Council, religious congregations were encouraged to return to the original inspiration of their founders, to study how this inspiration was articulated in the course of their histories. This was a vast, long-term project of accessing and cataloguing archives, in particular for those congregations whose archives were situated in different areas, either within individual countries or dispersed in various corners of the world. It required on-going planning in order to find a balance between centralising archival material internationally and retaining local archival material in parts of the world. This continues to be a work in progress. In their book, *Nano Nagle. The Life and the Legacy,* the authors have made a truly significant contribution to the history of the Presentations Sisters. They based their research on the archives of the congregation in Ireland and in those parts of the world where the congregation is located. A daunting task in terms of time and travel, research and writing.

The book begins with the life of the founder of the Presentation Sisters, Nano Nagle, 1718–1784. She was born into a prosperous Catholic gentry family, a family which had long roots in Ireland, indeed from Norman times. Down the centuries generations of the Nagles had been shaped by successive events, the Tudor and Stuart Plantations, the Reformation and then the Counter-Reformation. More closely to Nano's lifetime, the Nagle family was directly impacted by the defeat of James II at the Battle of the Boyne in 1690 and his subsequent exile in France, in St Germain-en-Laye. Nano's grand-uncle, Richard Nagle, was Secretary of War to James II and after the defeat joined the Court of James II in France. There he married and had a large family, which in time provided welcome space for visits from Irish members of the family. This included Nano, when she was sent to France to further her education. There she was brought into contact with several religious communities of women, among them the Ursulines. In time she would invite this community to Cork.

Life for the Nagle family in Ireland was burdened by the restrictions of the Penal Laws. Nano was acutely aware of the dire poverty in the Catholic community and wished to address this. From 1750, using her personal family wealth, she determined to provide schools for the poor girls and boys in Cork city. By 1769 she had set up five schools for girls and two schools for boys. This initial commitment to work with poor children in Cork led in time to her founding a new community, the Presentation Sisters. And yet, as *Nano Nagle. The Life and the Legacy* shows, she found her way, tentatively and even haphazardly, slowly, by trial and error, and often through what she did not want, until she struck out finally and independently. This independence was powerfully supported when she inherited vast wealth from her uncle. She invited a community of French Ursuline Sisters to come and establish a school for girls in Cork city, and she built accommodation both for the community and for the school.

However, Nano soon realised that the Ursuline community would focus only on the education of the Catholic middle class in Cork, because their rule of cloister prevented them from leaving their convent to work with the poor. This disappointment led to Nano's decision to found her own community on

Christmas Eve 1775, in Cove Lane, Cork, dedicated solely to the education of poor girls and boys. This community would be known as the Sisters of the Charitable Instruction of the Sacred Heart of Jesus. Then, rather in the style of Francis of Assisi, she cast about for a Rule of Life she could adapt to suit the purpose of her new community. Her work was almost done and her health was deteriorating. In 1783 she founded an asylum for older, destitute women. A year later she was dead.

The authors of *Nano Nagle. The Life and the Legacy* then turn to the legacy of Nano Nagle, as the community learnt to live without her strong presence. Gradually her early companions moved forward. By 1830 twenty-two communities were established in fourteen counties in Ireland. From these communities new foundations were made in Ireland and internationally. Details of the skills, inventiveness and doggedness of the communities are impressive, within situations which were often daunting and required money most new communities did not possess, either in Ireland or elsewhere.

There are several sub-texts in this book which the authors could not fully address, but they have provided many significant signposts to them. One sub-text concerns how Nano, in her lifetime, and her communities after her death, related to and were regarded by the institutional Church in Ireland and elsewhere. It would be enlightening to explore these experiences in the context of the Church in Ireland during the Penal Laws, then after Catholic Emancipation and prior to the First Vatican Council in 1870. That year the Church lost the Papal States and the Council passed the decree asserting papal infallibility. The Church turned inwards, measures were established to maintain discipline in the Church. Rules and regulations for women religious became more intrusive, especially after the publication of the Code of Canon Law in 1917, and this would have impacted on the Presentation Sisters.

Another related sub-text is the issue of religious freedom. This is particularly important in the case of Nano Nagle, who never set out to become a religious; she only made her final profession as a religious shortly before she died. Her personal independence was essential to the freedom of her spirit. It was a strange irony that the Ursuline community could not minister to the poor of Cork city, as Nano had hoped. Their founder, Angela Merici in the sixteenth century, had the same vision as Nano, to minister to the poor in their homes. Nevertheless, she was forced to accept strict cloister imposed on women religious by the Council of Trent. This pattern of seeking to curtail the freedom of women religious is repeated down the centuries and found in the life of Nano Nagle.

At the conclusion of their book, the authors indicate that further organisation, classification and cataloguing of historical material pertaining to the Presentation Sisters continues apace. In the course of this work new material and resources for future researchers will surely emerge. These will lead to further studies on Nano Nagle, on how her inspiration was taken on by those intrepid companions who knew her, and by those who were drawn later to join the Presentation Sisters. This book will remain an essential resource for researchers and serve as a well-constructed bridge to these future studies. This is the achievement of the three authors of this fine book.

Dr Phil Kilroy RSCJ is a historian and former provincial of her order in Ireland. Her *Madeleine Sophie Barat – A Life* was published by Cork University Press in 2000.

Women Writing War: Ireland 1880-1922, Tina O'Toole, Gillian McIntosh and Miriam O'Cinnéide (eds) (Dublin: UCD Press, 2016), 190 pages.

In their introduction, the editors explain that the objective of the book is to investigate the ways in which women's writing in and about Ireland conceptualises conflict in the period 1880–1922. These years include the Land War, the Second Boer War, the War of Independence, the First World War and the start of the Civil War. In addition to a preface by Margaret Ward, an introductory chapter by the three editors, an essay by Lia Mills on her 2014 play, *Fallen*, together with a short extract from the play, there are more than half-a-dozen chapters on women writers. The writers include Anna Parnell, Anna Blunt, Winfred Letts, Alice Stopford-Green, Eva Gore-Booth, Agnes O'Farrelly and Peggie Kelly, who wrote under the pseudonym of Garrett O'Driscoll.

All the essays are filled with interesting information and insights. The reader may be drawn to one or other according to taste. Only a flavour can be given here. Some women write poetry, some prose, some both. Some write in the Irish language as well as in English. Agnes O'Farrelly, a founder member and chairperson at the inaugural meeting of Cumann na mBan in April 1914, penned the first Irish language poetry collection to be published by a woman. This was *Áille an Domhain*, published in 1927. Her first poetry collection,

Out of the Depths, written in English, had been published a few years earlier in 1921. Rióna Nic Congáil, who writes the essay on O'Farrelly, says that it was only when Máire Mhac an tSaoi published a collection of poetry in Irish in the 1950s that critical attention began to be paid to women writing poetry in Irish.

When the National University was established in 1908, O'Farrelly obtained a job as lecturer in Irish in UCD. Among her students was Brian Ó Nualláin (Myles na gCopaleen). While unimpressed by her spoken Irish, Ó Nualláin described O'Farrelly as having 'a heart of gold'. Notwithstanding her qualities and ability, Nic Congáil says that she became 'a marginalised and ridiculed figure' because she saw the role of Cumann na mBan as occupying a subordinate position vis-à-vis the Volunteers. Hannah Sheehy-Skeffington remarked that 'Any society of women which proposes to act as "an animated collecting box" for men cannot have the sympathy of any self-respecting woman'. Inevitably, a split occurred in Cumann naBan.

Winifred Letts, an English-born writer who spent many years in Ireland, is the subject of an essay by Lucy Collins. Letts's father was an English clergyman and her mother was Irish. When her father died, she and her mother moved to Dublin where she attended Alexandra College. Letts is described as 'a prolific prose writer' and one of the few women to have had plays produced in the Abbey. She published two volumes of poetry in 1913 and 1926, entitled *Songs of Leinster* and *More Songs of Lenister.* Letts is probably best known for her war poems published in 1916, *Hallowe'en Poems of War*. Arguably Letts comes closest to satisfying the objective of the editors regarding how a woman writer 'conceptualises conflict' at this time. Letts does so in a compassionate way

Letts had worked as a Red Cross volunteer and witnessed in an intimate and immediate way, the human cost of war. One line captures the waste: 'The sheaves they bear for harvesting will be our garnered dead'. In the course of the war, any deserter would be shot without mercy – 'an English bullet in his heart'. Far from the heroics of war, Letts's compassionate insight into the soldier who does not 'measure up' is captured in a few lines in 'The Deserter':

> But who can judge him, you or I?
> God makes a man of flesh and blood
> Who yearns to live and not to die.

In her poem 'Chaplain to the Forces', Letts depicts chaplains at a distance from the dangers of the Front. This was not true in all cases, especially among Catholic chaplains. Among Irish Jesuit chaplains alone, four were killed at the Front.

The subject of Muireann O'Cinnéide's essay, Lady Anne Blunt, is also an Englishwoman. O'Cinnéide says that as 'an Englishwoman embroiled in Irish affairs, as Lord Byron's granddaughter, and as Wilfrid Scawen Blunt's wife, Lady Anne Blunt offers contemporary commentators a distinctive focal point for transnational correlations between anti-Imperial struggles'. There is mention of the couple's 'shared mutual love of travel, Arabian horses and of the East'. Perhaps it is not considered relevant to the theme, but there is no mention of the fact that Blunt rode through the Arabian desert and that one reason for the extensive travel in the Middle East by the Blunts was to purchase Arabian horses which they brought home to the renowned Crabbet Stud which they founded in England and which remained in operation until the 1970s. Details of Blunt's travels were recorded in her journals, subsequently published as books. Augusta Gregory, we are told, became passionately involved with Wilfrid Blunt. Gregory described Anna as 'the epitome of vulnerable marital loyalty'. One is permitted to ask if talented, independent women from Anne Blunt to Norma Major, to Mary Archer, even Hillary Clinton, fall into the category of 'vulnerable marital loyalty'?

Emily Lawless is the subject of an essay by Heidi Hansson. Lawless who is best known for her poem 'After Aughrim', was an environmentalist who mourned the loss of trees and forests. The daughter of Lord Cloncurry, she explicitly says 'war writing belongs to the masculine domain'. In her Diary of the Boer War, *A Garden Diary 1899–1900,* she relates developments in her garden to developments in the war. Lawless, a Unionist, identifies with the British.

Tina O'Toole writes about a group of women supporters of Roger Casement in the essay entitled 'The New Women of the Glens: Writers and Revolutionaries'. These include Gertrude Bannister, Ada O'Neill and Alice Milligan. These women are described by O'Toole as part of a generation of newly empowered, educated, active and radical women. They 'openly professed first-wave feminist ambitions and were engaged in public discourse and social activism of one kind or another'. In a different world were Peggie Kelly and her sisters, who were brought up by the Dominican nuns in a boarding school in Kingstown (Dun Laoghaire) when, first their mother, then their father who was a ship's captain, died while the children were young.

Peggie Kelly wrote under a male pseudonym while her sister Frances (Judy) was a fine artist who won the Taylor scholarship at the College of Art. Frances is the mother of Eavan Boland.

For the most part the writers are drawn from fairly privileged backgrounds, Protestant and Catholic. Some women encountered obstacles and criticism – criticism sometimes proffered by other women. Such was the case when the work of the Ladies' Land League led by Anna Parnell was heavily criticised by the feminist *Englishwoman's Review,* as told by Diane Urquhart in her essay on Parnell. Faced with the eviction of poor families from the land, the Ladies' Land League had spread to England where branches were set up to raise awareness and support among Irish emigrants. The president of the London Branch was Frances Sullivan, who later would be a founding member of the Pioneer Total Abstinence Association (PTTA) which was started by the Irish Jesuit James Cullen. Cullen was someone who placed a high value on the contribution of women. In the early years of the PTTA, membership was confined to women, as Cullen believed that 'women have been the world's greatest social reformers'. It was not until 1986, years after Anna Parnell's death, that her book *Tales of a Great Sham*, about the Ladies' Land League, was published.

Women Writing War testifies to the spectrum of beliefs held by women writers from the more traditional to the more emancipated. Whatever their stance, there is no doubt that the women made a significant contribution at a time when, in the words of Alice Stopford-Green, 'the feminine as opposed to the masculine are becoming more and more decisive in human affairs'. Nonetheless, despite obstacles and antagonisms faced by the women writers in this fine collection, those obstacles were probably less daunting than the ones faced by an impoverished man, Sean O'Casey.

Dr Finola Kennedy is an economist.
Her *Frank Duff: A Life Story* was published in 2011.

The Coming of the Celts, AD 1860: Celtic Nationalism in Ireland and Wales, Caoimhín De Barra (Notre Dame: University of Notre Dame Press, 2018), 372 pages.

Caoimhín De Barra's *The Coming of the Celts* is a well-considered examination of the often-ambivalent relationship between the respective promoters of Welsh and Irish language, literature and culture in the later nineteenth and earlier twentieth centuries. De Barra, a member of the History Faculty at Gonzaga University in Spokane, Washington, sees the language movements in Wales and Ireland both as part of the general development of romantic bourgeois nationalism that flourished among smaller, or divided, nationalities in nineteenth-century Europe and also as an often-failed attempt to discover political and cultural commonalities between the two countries, and the other Celtic nations, commonalities that sometimes simply didn't exist.

There were two significant fault lines separating the Welsh and Irish language movements. The first was mutual unintelligibility between speakers of the two major divisions among the six modern Celtic languages, the Goidelic languages (Irish and Scottish Gaelic, descended from a high Medieval form of Irish – two languages that are mutually understandable) and the Brittonic languages (Welsh and Breton, descended from a Celtic language spoken in Wales and West Britain in late antiquity – languages that are unintelligible both to speakers of the Goidelic languages and to speakers of the two major Brittonic tongues). Two other Celtic languages, Cornish (a Brittonic language) and Manx (a Goidelic language), died out, primarily in the eighteenth century (with remnants of Manx surviving until a few generations ago), but these languages recently have been revived as sometimes precocious hobby-languages by scholars and enthusiasts, through the examination of historic texts.

While older 'Irish' and 'Welsh' thus are the primary historic progenitors of their respective modern language groups, these two languages developed mostly in isolation from one another and thus proved poor vehicles for a unified 'Celtic' consciousness and collective cultural/political programmes. Such programmes preoccupied a relatively small number of Pan-Celtic supporters in the late nineteenth and early twentieth centuries, but their goals usually were hazy and unrealisable – the product of collective undefined goodwill as much as anything. Also, five of the six modern Celtic nations had

English as a well-established first language by the period in question, which tended to isolate the Bretons, who often were among the more enthusiastic of the Pan-Celts. Finally, while the later Gaelic League in Ireland had a political and cultural programme that was decidedly Modernist and forward-looking, attempting to update the Irish language in contemporary settings, the Scottish, Welsh and Breton Pan-Celts too often (to the Irish, at least) seemed preoccupied with a 'Golden' past and too concerned with externals like Druidical ceremonies and national costumes.

A second point of division, one repeatedly alluded to by De Barra but never considered in sufficient depth, was religious. Welsh speakers during the time in question were largely evangelical Calvinistic Methodist dissenters, extremely suspicious of Roman Catholicism, while members of the Irish language movement were mostly (at least cultural) Catholics. This religious division led to suspicion and a certain cultural revulsion between the two groups, more often coming from the Welsh than the Irish side of things, which sometimes proved a difficulty in efforts at mutual programmatic development. Both 'primordial' languages, however, survived periods of significant religious change in the twentieth century, with the Welsh national conversion from Protestant evangelicalism to the increasingly secular socialism of the Labour Party; and the general Irish detachment from Catholicism after the clerical sexual-abuse crisis of the late twentieth and early twenty-first centuries.

The development of the nationalist impulse in each of the four major Celtic nations during the last half of the nineteenth century went hand-in-hand with a movement toward pan-Celtic appreciation, if not unity, perhaps inspired by the example of Italian and German unification. This impulse, while recurring and popular on the surface, ultimately was a failure. While there might have been distant linguistic connections between the two primary Celtic-language groups somewhere on the continent of Europe, their existence in proximity to one another in Britain and Ireland during later antiquity and the Medieval period was to a considerable degree coincidental – the result of population shifts both on the continent and within Britain and Ireland, over which some of the players had little control.

Nonetheless, the resurgence of national sensibilities, replete with mythic 'rediscoveries', in the later nineteenth century seemingly was irresistible, in the 'Celtic' nations, as elsewhere in Europe, and a number of cultural organisations were formed (some of which quickly disintegrated) during the period in question to advance both 'national' and Pan-Celtic agendas. The Celtic Federal Union was proposed 1921–1923 by the Welsh politician and Pan-Celt promoter Edward Thomas John (1857–1931). The Gaelic League was founded in 1893 to promote Irish language and literature, thereafter with a somewhat ambivalent attitude toward the rest of the Celtic world. Douglas Hyde (1860–1949), Patrick Pearse (1879–1916) and Eóin MacNeill (1867–1954) were, however, supportive of Pan-Celtic efforts. Various Pan-Celtic Congresses were organised – in 1901 and 1925 in Dublin; in 1904 in Caernarfon; in 1907 and 1920 in Edinburgh; in 1921 in the Isle of Man; and in 1924 in Brittany. Thereafter, the Pan-Celtic impulse dissipated with the establishment of the Irish Free State in 1922, which many Pan-Celts saw as a watershed event but also as a confusing one – should the goals of Pan-Celticism thereafter be first political, like the Irish, or cultural, like the Welsh? Some of the early Pan-Celtic efforts were indeed Irish-centred, like the Pan-Celtic Society (1888–1891). The fact that early Irish Pan-Celtic efforts sometimes were led by 'unrepresentative' members of the Protestant Ascendency class (e.g. Bernard FitzPatrick, 2nd Baron Castletown, 1848–1937; and Edmund Edward Fournier d'Albe, 1868–1933) sometimes rendered Pan-Celtic efforts as suspect in the eyes of rank-and-file Catholic Irish nationalists.

The earliest of the Pan-Celts were antiquarians like the Scot George Buchanan (1506–1582), the Breton Paul-Ives Pezron (1639–1706), and the Welsh-descended Edward Lhuyd (1660–1709), who speculated about the history and languages of disparate European peoples, which they believed possibly were inter-related groups, groups that they began sparingly to describe collectively as 'Celts' or 'Celtic'. The works of these individuals, and others, including authors of romantic speculation, were 'codified' by Teutonic and other scholars as the nineteenth century wore on, so that by the turn of the century, the study of the modern Celtic languages, and of the history of 'Celtic' peoples, individually and collectively, both were well-established, if still on somewhat tentative scholarly grounds.

A great debate among the Welsh and Irish during this time concerned which of the two languages was more vital and actually 'alive'. Then as now, Welsh was more often the first spoken language among Welsh people than Gaelic was among the Irish, although the goal to revive Gaelic as a viable language, a movement generated during this period, proved, over time, after considerable heroic effort, to be a moderate success. About 19% of the Welsh today count Welsh as their first language, with 29% of the Welsh population claiming some Welsh-language skills; comparable figures for Ireland as a whole are 1.2% and 28%. Breton today is regularly spoken by only about 5% of the population of Brittany – down considerably from approximately 25% in 1950 (the French like the British historically had, until recently, used the coercive power of government to reduce the influence of certain local cultures). Scottish Gaelic is spoken as a first language by approximately 1.1% of the Scottish population, with 1.6% claiming some Scots-Gaelic skills. Wales and Ireland, in different ways, thus are the clear 'successes' in the general movement toward Celtic language preservation. (The percentages recorded here are taken from recent census records).

A number of elements bound Wales to Britain more tightly than was true of Ireland in the early twentieth century – a healthy long-standing cultural insularity, tolerated by Britain, constituting the main element in this. For instance, David Lloyd George, a native Welsh speaker, was the British Prime Minister, 1916–1922, and exemplified Welsh participation in the British political system; the Welsh focused their political ambitions not through a 'Home Rule' party like the Irish Parliamentary Party or Sinn Féin (although many Welsh people supported the notion of Welsh autonomy and a local legislature), but rather primarily (until recently) through the Liberal and later Labour parties, which were 'British' Parties; the Welsh educational system had accommodated Welsh-speakers long before the idea of teaching Irish in Ireland's primary and secondary schools was seriously considered (probably because the Welsh were Protestants and thus not considered a potential political threat like Irish Catholics); the significant periodical literature in Welsh (much more plentiful than in Irish) tended to support the status quo; and, finally, most of the Welsh were highly critical of revolutionary political violence and viewed the 1916 Rising with hostility (while generally treating Irish POWS with kindness when they were housed in Welsh prisons or camps).

In very general terms, residents of the six modern Celtic nations were and are proud to be described individually and collectively as 'Celts', to share a somewhat indistinct collective identity forged during the period covered in de Barra's book, and to acknowledge one another as Celtic 'cousins', but all are today more or less contented to leave it at that and not pursue any imperial role for Pan-Celticism.

De Barra should be credited with writing a clear, nuanced, detailed account of a complex subject, the features of which this review can only briefly highlight. His book is recommended to any library or reader with an interest in the history, language, literature, and folk-lore of the six modern Celtic nations.

Dr John B Davenport is retired Professor of History at North Central University in Minneapolis, Minnesota.

Waterford Merchants and their Families on Distant Shores: Traders in Spain and France from 1600 to 1800, Liam Murphy (Blackrock: Kingdom Books, 2019), 288 pages.

Waterford was the second most important city in Ireland for hundreds of years after the Norman invasion, due to its extensive trading links with the continent. After the Cromwellian conquest, the city's ruling Catholic merchants were forced to leave, having lost their right to trade and to hold civic positions. These emigrant merchants and their descendants set up trading houses in the port cities of France, Spain and the Spanish Netherlands and many of them were remarkably successful in both trade and public life. Most were members of the Old English Catholic merchant class who dominated the city before the Cromwellian invasion. Some of them had set up trading posts on the continent well before Cromwell arrived in Ireland, but it was the brutal and anti-Catholic nature of the settlement in the 1650s that forced them to leave. Not only did they lose their power in Waterford – they lost the right to trade as merchants.

The loyalty of so many of the Old English to Catholicism was a remarkable feature of seventeenth century Ireland. These people were loyal to the crown, but were not prepared to abandon their religion and instead chose persecution and the loss of everything they possessed. Among the common surnames of the merchants who fled the city at this time were Aylward, Comerford, Fitzgerald, Power, Walsh and White.

Descendants of the initial emigrants had remarkable careers on the continent. Antoine Walsh, a slave trader in Nantes, brought Bonnie Prince Charlie to Scotland for the ill-fated Jacobite rebellion of 1745. Nicolas Geraldino (Fitzgerald) from Cadiz commanded the Spanish flagship in the Spanish/French victory over the British at Toulon during the war of the Austrian Succession. Other truly remarkable people among the Waterford families included Jose Blanco White, a well known writer and indefatigable controversialist, who changed his religion twice, beginning life as a Catholic, converting to Anglicanism and ending as a Unitarian. Maria Gertrudis Hore, described as the most beautiful woman in the Cadiz of her day, was a leading writer in Spain in the eighteenth century.

Liam Murphy tells the fascinating story of these Waterford families. His extensive research is based on a wide variety of sources in Spanish and French, as well as English. The book throws light on a hidden part of our history which deserves to be much more widely known. It begins by tracing the history of Waterford from its foundation by the Vikings to the establishment of a thriving continental trade in the late Middle Ages. Most of the wine imported into the country at this period came through Waterford.

The real focus is what happens from the mid-seventeenth century onwards, as the Waterford merchant families were forced into exile in order to continue trading. They were astonishingly successful in this endeavour, establishing thriving businesses in Malaga, Cadiz, Seville, Tenerife, La Coruña, Bilbao, St Malo, Nantes, Bordeaux, La Rochelle, Ostend and Bruges.

As the families put down roots around the continent, they began to take part in the public and religious life of their adopted countries. Major figures like Cardinal Nicholas Wiseman and Cardinal Rafael Merry del Val were of Waterford descent. In 1850 Pius IX re-established the Catholic hierarchy in England and appointed Wiseman as Cardinal Archbishop of Westminster, the first cardinal to reside in England since the Reformation. Cardinal Merry del Val served in the Vatican as secretary of state from 1903 to 1914 and as secretary of the Congregation of the Holy Office from 1914 to 1930. At a more conventional level, many of the descendants of the Waterford merchants had distinguished careers in the Spanish and French armed forces. Antoine Walsh, who was descended from two Waterford families, served in the French navy and thereafter, in the 1720s, settled in Nantes, then the hub of the Atlantic slave-trade.

This trade was triangular in nature, with manufactured goods such as textiles, brandy and firearms being transported to Africa, where they were traded for African slaves. The slaves were then transported across the Atlantic to the French West Indian colonies of Martinique, Guadeloupe and Saint-Dominque (now Haiti), where they were in turn sold for sugar and tobacco for the European market. Antoine first served as a slave-ship captain, before becoming a wealthy slave-merchant.

Most of the Waterford merchants on distant shores engaged in more conventional trade in goods like wine and textiles and were remarkably successful in their commercial enterprises. Some were immensely wealthy by the standards of the time and they made generous donations to charitable works and the Church in Spain and in Waterford. Others exerted influence in the royal courts of Europe.

One of the main reasons for the success of the Waterford merchant families was their attachment to the Catholic faith they shared with the people of their adopted countries. Many of the families retained links with Waterford down the generations. It is timely in the era of Brexit to be reminded of the connections that tied one Irish city to the wider world for so long. The author is to be commended for conducting research in a variety of languages and presenting his fascinating research is such a readable form.

Stephen Collins recently retired as Political Editor of *The Irish Times*, to which he continues to contribute on a regular basis.

SUBSCRIPTION
Subscribe to *Studies*, An Irish Quarterly Review

Send completed form to: **Studies, 37 Lower Leeson Street, Dublin 2, Ireland**
or subscribe online at: **www.studiesirishreview.ie**
or email Vera at: **studies@jesuit.ie**
or telephone Vera on: **+353 1 6767491 to pay by credit card**

I wish to subscribe / renew my subscription to *Studies*

Area	One Year	Two Years	Three Years
Ireland	€45	€80	€115
Britain	€55	€100	€145
EU/ROW	€50	€90	€130

Name_____

Address_____

_____

Ph/ Email: _____

For Credit Card Payments:

Card Type: Visa ☐ MasterCard ☐ Maestro ☐ Laser ☐

Card Number: /__ __ __ __ /__ __ __ __ /__ __ __ __ /__ __ __ __

Expiry Date: /__ __ /__ __ Amount : €_____

Cardholder's Name: _____

Billing Address:_____

_____

Recipient's Name and Address (if different from your own)

Name: _____

Address: _____

_____